AF226319

BEYOND MY UNDERSTANDING

*My life
during and after
Jehovah's Witnesses*

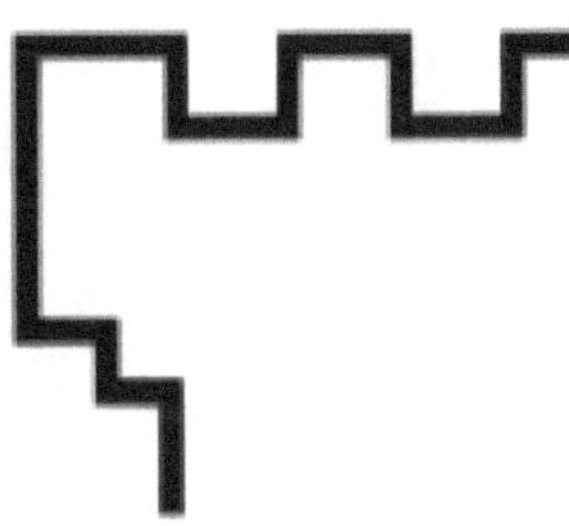

GAIL SHARPE KELLY

Beyond My Understanding

A memoir:

My life during and after Jehovah's Witnesses

Gail Sharpe Kelly

Copyright © 2019, Gail Sharpe Kelly

All Rights Reserved.

Print Edition

Cover design by Sara Carrick

This is a memoir. A number of names of people and places have been changed to protect parties who may have played a role in the author's true memories.

This book is dedicated with love and gratitude to:
the memory of Ronald William Kelly
on our life journey together;
the memory of my
Great Aunt Margaret Armstrong
McConkey (Barclay) Marshall
for her support in every way;
my grandson Mathew Liam Kelly
for his inspiration when I was at my lowest.
His presence kept me moving forward.

~Chapter One~

The strange thing about memory is that it is often selective. It can seem like the moment was only yesterday, presented with crystal clarity, and yet at times it can prove unreliable.

In one of my earliest clear memories, I was a child, playing in our yard on a fall day. I recall the smell of leaves on the ground, a cool breeze and a feeling of autumn in the air.

Our family was making a fuss over the new baby, just home from the hospital. Everyone was gathered in our small insole brick house: my mother, father, mother's sister Audrey and my new baby brother, Kenneth John Sharpe.

To tell the truth, I was feeling jealous about all the attention the baby was receiving. The entire family was ignoring me. I remember thinking, "I'll fix them. I'll run away." I saw some children walking near my fence on their way to school and decided to follow them. A school crossing guard was manning a busy intersection near our home, taking the children across the road.

I followed them to the school yard, which I later came to know was Norman Cook Junior Public School, on Danforth Road near St. Clair Avenue. I must have realized I would not be able to enter the school, as I was too young and not enrolled. I heard the bell ring and watched the children leave the playground and go inside.

I decided to knock on the door of a house near the school. When a lady answered the door, I told her I was hungry and asked for some candy.

She invited me in and sat me down with milk and cookies. I don't recall her face.

It was September, 1953. I was three and a half years old.

I was surprised to hear a description of myself on the radio. The police were looking for me. I'd decided to leave the house when the lady said, "Would you like some jelly beans?"

She busied me with the candy and called the radio station.

I did my best to ignore her phone call and focus on eating the sweets.

The next thing I remember is my Dad driving up to the house in the old truck he had at the time, knocking on the door and coming inside.

When we arrived home, my mother was crying and very angry. I received a good spanking for running away. She told me I'd been a bad girl for scaring her, and ordered me to "Never do that again!"

I'd learned my lesson. I never did that again.

These memories are vivid and deeply ingrained in my mind.

For the most part, my early memories are sporadic. What I do recall is a mixed bag at best, and not always reliable.

The clearest memories are from between the ages of four and seven years. When I was very small, I was at a grocery store and asked my mother for a chocolate bar.

She said no.

In my childish wisdom, I decided if I grabbed a bar, she would have no choice but to pay for it.

Once we were out of the store, my mother saw me with the chocolate bar and asked me where I'd gotten it. I told her, and she proceeded to bring me back inside the store, demanding that I give it back and apologize for stealing it.

I was so ashamed, I wished I could disappear. I will tell you this: I never stole another thing in my life.

My parents instilled good values of honesty. They did not favour any particular race. They loved all people and taught me to put kindness first, to always be polite. They emphasized honesty in all life's decisions. They did their best to teach me to live a good life and to be a good person in all my affairs.

Theirs was a simple basic guiding principle: Follow the Golden Rule. I believe they would have done that even if they had not taken up with the Jehovah's Witnesses, because that's who they were, honest and hard-working. They had been raised with that same principle.

I found a picture of myself as a baby, celebrating Christmas with my Great Aunt Margaret, Great Aunt Kathleen (Kit), paternal grandmother Eleanor Elizabeth Zeta (Barclay) Sharpe Parker and her second husband John Parker, as well as my mother and father. The year was 1951.

That must have been the last time my parents celebrated Christmas. I can't find any other pictures with a tree or other holiday indicators.

My life changed forever when a Jehovah's Witness came to our door. That's how my mother got involved in the JW religion, and eventually convinced my father to join as well.

I believe Dad was resistant at first. I don't know what changed his mind, or why he chose to convert.

I never had a choice as to whether I wanted to follow this religion. I was just raised in it. All I remember is not being able to go to parties, or to attend any functions related to Christmas, Halloween, Easter or birthday parties. Everything was off limits.

Other children who might have been friends were also off limits. I was only permitted to associate with other JW children, children of "the faith" or "the truth", as they referred to their religion. I was told they were the true Christians. Everyone else was Pagan or Heathen and I was not allowed to associate with them.

There were a number of unbending rules involved in our new faith. We did not take blood or blood transfusions, because of our interpretation of the Bible. Needless to say, I did not enjoy a social life. My world revolved around attending meetings, book studies, going door-to-door, appearing on stage at the Kingdom Hall, or performing in skits on how to approach people who were not indoctrinated in the Jehovah Witness faith.

We were taught how to approach people, how to convince them to purchase our literature, or to accept it for free and most important, to read it. The JWs believed we were preaching God's will.

As a child, I went along with the religion. Like most very young children, I believed my parents knew everything, and so I did as I was told. My parents sheltered me from others, especially those who were not Witnesses, which was pretty much everyone in our neighborhood.

So I followed what my parents ordered, like so many young people before me. That's what we do. At least until we grow up and start asking questions.

Eventually, if you've been blessed with a brain, the questions will come.

I was always inquisitive. Because my brother had red hair and I was a brunette, I worried that we might have been adopted! I remember asking my parents that very question. Of course they denied it, and showed me my birth certificate.

The point is that I was questioning things, even in those early days, because things did not seem to make sense.

There were good memories, mixed in among the more rigid recollections. Some of the fondest ones were of being at our cottage. My Great Aunt Margaret had a place not far from ours on Orr Lake. I recall swimming for hours, and playing on the sandy beach.

Most days, my mother would have to call me out of the lake for dinner. One meal in particular stands out in memory: roast chicken, mashed potatoes, gravy and dumplings. My mother was an excellent cook!

I also recall enjoying hot baths in an old galvanized steel washtub. It felt so good, warm, soothing and comforting. Our lives were simple then, in the 1950s.

Too bad those days didn't last.

I'm grateful for those wonderful memories. Without them, I'd have very little to show in life. So thanks for the memories! No one else could know how truly swell it felt. It was fantastic. I always knew I was loved and cared for as a small child.

One day, while playing in the sand, I was stung by a hive of wasps which had nested in the ground. I was rushed to the nearest hospital.

I have a photograph in my collection of myself playing in the sand at Orr Lake. Back then, any household item could be used as a toy. In this picture, I'm using an oil can and a spoon as a shovel. I sure look like I was enjoying myself, with long ringlets hanging down around my face. I was a cute and very happy little girl.

Do I look as though I cared whether my toys were not a real pail or shovel?

When any of you parents out there are thinking you have to buy all kinds of expensive toys for your children, take heed: you do not. Children need very little to be truly happy and content. They don't require their parents to constantly make a big deal, or to try to keep them busy. Given the chance, children can busy themselves.

Let them play in the sand. Let them be children.

They'll have plenty of time to become adults.

My Uncle Max was not a blood relative, but was a friend of my mother's from her younger years. My parents would enjoy lively discussions with Uncle Max, and they appreciated his ideas and points of view on religion.

In 1954 I was four years old. I was recovering from a hernia surgery, and was having difficulty walking. Uncle Max carried me down the road for an ice cream cone.

Afterward, he refused to carry me, insisting I walk back to the house.

Of course, I cried, saying it hurt too much to walk and begging him to carry me.

He reminded me that we'd had a deal. He would carry me to the store, but I would have to walk back.

Each step was painful, but soon it became easier, and before long the pain was barely noticeable. Soon, there was no slowing me down. I was back to my old self, and no longer needed to be carried.

Uncle Max was a smart man, and good with children. He had a kind manner. He said what he meant, and he meant what he said. I respected him for that.

He got me walking again, when my parents were at their wits end, unable to get me back on my feet. I know they were happy and grateful to him.

The JWs had a slogan: Keep Your Eyes on the Prize. Of course, they were referring to a New World or Kingdom.

I was just thinking about the ice cream cone!

I also had my tonsils and adenoids removed. I remember running out of the hospital room before that operation and begging my Dad to take me home. The place smelled of ether and antiseptic. My father brought me back to the room, saying I needed to have the procedure.

I went through a lot as a small child, and those memories are vivid.

When I was not yet four, I desperately wanted to take ballet class for preschool. Soon after joining, I changed my mind. I felt so clumsy and shy. I felt truly uncomfortable and was convinced I was terrible at ballet. I left the room, telling my mother I didn't want to take lessons after all.

My mother was angry. She felt I'd wasted her time and money, signing up for something and not following it through. I lacked confidence.

Now, many years later, I understand the reasons why I suffered such low self-esteem. I didn't like sports. I felt inept at everything.

My mother responded by saying, "Don't ever ask me to sign you up for anything ever again. I won't do it." She was not the world's most understanding mother.

She got along much better with my brother, Kenneth, than with me.

I think it was because he shared her interest in sports. Or maybe it was just a "mother and son" bond, being able to relate more easily to the male child.

By 1956 we were living at 7 Marsh Road. I remember coming home from school. I would have been about six years old.

I arrived home to find my mother about to rush Kenneth to the hospital. My three-year-old brother had swallowed pills, either diet pills or sleeping aids. He needed his stomach pumped.

Ken had climbed onto the kitchen counter looking for gum. He didn't believe my mother when she told him there wasn't any. Thinking the pills were gum, he ate them.

He spent the night in the hospital.

Our house on Marsh Road was a duplex, attached to another matching brick house.

From there, we moved to 74 Blakemanor Blvd. in Scarborough, Ontario, Canada. The new house was a bungalow. I was seven when we moved, and Ken was four.

The new house was built from the ground up, so our move was delayed for a while.

One day, our parents took us to see the unfinished house. As we got out of the car, Dad slammed the door, not noticing that Mom's hand was in the way.

Her pain was terrible! She screamed, of course. Dad felt terrible and was doing his best to pry the car door open to free Mom's hand.

She refused to go to the hospital, despite the rending pain. Instead, we went into the basement of the new house and put cold water from the laundry taps onto her hand.

At the time, I thought it strange that she wouldn't allow us to take her to the hospital. But I didn't think too much about it. As children, we tend to go with the flow.

Now, thinking back, I realize my mother was too independent for her own good.

It was ridiculous, really. At the times when she most needed help, she would not allow anyone to care for her.

To this day, I have no idea what made her that way.

~Chapter Two~

I was a lonely child.

The reasons for my loneliness were a mystery to me.

My brother, Ken, was always out playing with the neighborhood children. He would disappear whenever it was time to attend a JW meeting.

If the meeting was scheduled to be at our house, he was nowhere to be found.

As an adolescent, I was furious that he was able to get away with taking off in that way.

Our parents did punish Ken, but it was never severe and it never stuck. He just kept up his defiant ways.

My mother's illness probably had a lot to do with their lenience toward him. He was only fifteen when our Mom died.

I was quiet, and had a habit of talking to myself. I would imagine being someone else, and visiting strange places. Someone took a photo of me sitting in my brother's wagon in the back yard. I'd just finished having one of those conversations with myself. It was indicative of how very alone I felt. When they approached me and accused me of talking to myself, I denied it, embarrassed.

The society my parents raised me in was a deeply isolated one. It was a world apart, one filled with Meetings, Bible Studies and Conventions, or Assemblies. It involved going door-to-door, preaching the Good News, as we called it. I'm sure my parents felt they were doing the right thing, raising us that way. They probably saw it as the best alternative.

I strongly disagree.

In my opinion, there are countless better ways to raise a child. Ways that will not cause them to spend their lives feeling isolated. I believe that no one religion or cult has the right to dictate to people how to think or act, or to impose on a child their way of life.

What I "witnessed" was a type of brainwashing, forcing people to listen to the same thing over and over again, and isolating them from other people and influences.

As a young Jehovah's Witness, you are not permitted to ask questions about the religion. You are simply forced to do as you are told.

Obedience is the constant order of the day.

I do not believe there is one correct religion. I believe in a Higher Power, God, but I think he can be found anywhere, not only in a church or Kingdom Hall. I believe he is wherever we seek him, and that God is there for everyone.

All we need do is ask for help. God will speak to us when we are open to Him.

I've found both good and bad people in many different religions. None are perfect, nor do they hold all the answers.

My second grade teacher was Mrs. A. She spoke with a Scottish brogue. In Cedarbrook Public School, she convinced me to participate in Highland dancing as well as square dancing on stage, to entertain on parents' and teachers' night.

I was part of a group of student dancers. I did quite well, but I recall that Mom never praised me. Dad said I did well. But not a word from Mom.

That lack of encouragement leaves a mark on a child. We may not realize it at the time, but in later years, we often come to understand the ways in which it has an impact.

Prior to this dancing incident, I had attended Scarborough Village Public School. My teacher there, Mrs. B., was truly awful. I recall how she ignored me when I put my hand up to go to the washroom. Finally, I could no longer hold my water and was forced to wet my pants. Mrs. B., in her cruelty, made me sit in my wet pants till school ended. I had to walk home like that.

When I told my mother what had happened, she went ballistic. She went straight to the school and gave Mrs. B. hell! Of course, the teacher apologized to my mother, but the damage was done. I was thoroughly humiliated in front of my classmates.

Needless to say, I hated that teacher.

At times like that, my mother was supportive. But there were contradictory actions on her part, seemingly related to our religion, that I never fully understood.

One really absurd thing happened in October, 1957. Despite the rules of the JW religion, my parents held a Halloween party for us in our unfinished basement.

Of course, we were not allowed to celebrate Halloween, and we were forbidden from Trick-or-Treating with the neighborhood children.

But they made this allowance, and we were permitted to invite classmates home after school for the party.

I was about seven at the time.

What kind of mixed message were our parents sending to my brother and me? No wonder I spent most of my childhood confused. I still don't know why they allowed it.

No one ever discussed the party. No one asked questions. They never did it again.

Actually, not talking openly about things was pretty common back then. People didn't discuss their feelings. Especially we children, we were to be seen and never heard. If we spoke out loud, we were considered rude. That was true at the time for most families, not only for ours.

We were the Baby Boomer generation!

Another very strange contradiction occurred, also in 1957. My father took my brother and me to Cedarbrae Mall. He arranged for us to have our picture taken with Santa Claus. He also took us to a Christmas party at his work, at the Post Office. I received a gift of a caramel coloured purse. It looked like a camera case. I don't recall what gift Ken was given.

More mixed messages. I never asked my father why he chose to make this exception. But he never did it again.

Despite the unwritten rules against asking questions, I was always inquisitive. And I was not against making things up, if it suited my needs at the time.

I must have been desperate to make friends. One day at school, I stood up in front of the whole class and invited them to my house for a party. I believed that once they arrived, my parents would back me up. I thought they would buy party food and make everyone welcome, because I'd made the commitment.

I was wrong. When my classmates arrived, I was forced to admit there was no party, and to send them home. I was humiliated and felt sorry for myself. I don't have any memory of the aftermath at school. Most likely I have blocked it out.

~Chapter Three~

My brother and I were at the cottage, out on the lake in our leaky row boat. We were constantly removing water with a can. We had no life jackets. Mind you, the lake wasn't that deep, but it was deep enough for fishing, and we were having fun pulling in sun fish and lazing around in the boat.

Oh to be a kid in the '50s! Just to enjoy a beautiful summer day and life in general!

It was the little things that gave us the most pleasure, like the taste of coca cola, or ginger ale or orange soda. It all seemed to taste better back then. My parents kept the pop and beer in the spring to keep it cold.

Our property was at the top of a hill at Orr Lake. The spring was in the middle of the property, on the way to the lake.

I recall pumping water from our spring-fed well. I remember priming the pump. Maybe it was imagination, but even the water tasted better, colder and fresher.

In many ways, I think people were happier in those simpler times. At least that seemed true in our family, and at our cottage. We enjoyed simple things, and easy living.

Maybe the cottage provided an escape from the city and our religion. I often wish I could ask my parents about that.

In the summer of 1959, my school held a contest. We were given seeds. The idea was to grow a garden and try to win a prize for the best garden of the summer.

My parents encouraged me to do my best, and they helped out with watering the garden.

I won second prize: $2.00.

Well, you'd think I'd won the lottery, based on how pleased my parents were! I was allowed to buy anything I wanted. I chose a peach-coloured short sleeved sweater.

It was a big deal to buy clothing from the store, as my mother made most of my clothes, or I received hand-me-downs.

There is nothing wrong with handed down or homemade clothes, but this was a special treat!

I was also given a trip to the Royal Agricultural Winter Fair at the Canadian Exhibition, to see the harvest of fruits and vegetables, as well as the livestock. It was very exciting for me. The place seemed large and full of adventure.

An old photograph dated August, 1959 reminds me of this period, as well as a home-perm hair style I wore then.

At the time, home-perms were common, something mothers did for their daughters.

In 1964, at the age of 14, I went to the movies with a girlfriend. We both tried to smoke cigarettes. I disliked the taste, and felt terribly guilty for doing it. I gave the pack to my friend, and stopped smoking. I suppose I'd just wanted to fit in somehow.

My parents didn't smoke, and it was frowned on in our religious community. I later learned that both of my parents had been smokers when they'd met in 1941.

In my mementos, I found a letter I'd started to write to my cousin in 1965.

At the time I had a crush on a fellow JW member. Members referred to themselves as being "in the Truth". I don't know if I ever sent the letter.

I'd just returned from a Convention in Peterborough. I'd gone with Dad and some other Jehovah's Witness members and must have met this fellow there.

I also volunteered at a Jehovah's Witness Convention at the Canadian National Exhibition (CNE) in 1966. My father encouraged me to volunteer, reminding me that my friend was also participating.

I was 16 years old. My memory of the day is sketchy. But somehow we had our picture taken and ended up featured in the *Toronto Star*. It was kind of a big deal for me and my friend from the Kingdom Hall, but I never did get a copy of the *Star* photo.

When I was 16, Great Aunt Margaret took us out to dinner in Barrie, at the Lakeview Dairy Restaurant. We were staying at the Orr Lake cottage that July, and would have driven south to meet in Barrie.

My mother was unwell in July of 1966, and she'd stayed home in Scarborough. So the dinner party was made up of Dad, my brother Ken, myself, and Aunt Margaret.

After dinner, Aunt Margaret tried stopping with us at several homes to visit, but no one was home. Finally, we all arrived at a house in Lefroy, in Simcoe, Ontario, a small village not far from Barrie.

Aunt Margaret knocked on the door, and Mina Janet (Constable) Kelly welcomed us in for tea. We were enjoying our refreshments when suddenly a young man in khaki coveralls appeared.

Mina introduced us to her son, Ronald William Kelly. I was immediately attracted to him, and I later learned the feeling was mutual.

Ron's dad, William Hugh Kelly, known as Bill, was also there, but I don't recall seeing him.

It was night time. Frank Sinatra was on the radio, singing "Strangers in the Night". It was the perfect setup for romance.

Bill later told us you could see the sparks flying when Ron and I met.

Ron asked me to go for a walk. We went to see his Dad's cedar boat at the marina on Lake Simcoe. He asked me whether I knew how we were related. I said I thought it was a distant relationship.

He asked me out on a date, my first date ever. The plan was for him to pick me up at our cottage on Orr Lake and take me to a Drive-In movie in Barrie. I accepted.

I wore a red and white polka dot dress with white high heels.

The dress had an open back, and went in at the waist with a full skirt. I had a white sweater.

It may not have been the right thing to wear to a Drive-In movie, but I looked and felt good, except for being very nervous.

We kissed, a lot, but that was as far as we went.

Ron told me he was planning to move to Toronto. He would be attending Radio College of Canada to study electronics and would visit me a lot.

So this is how our love affair began. And the rest, as they say, is history!

My parents did not approve. Ron was not a Jehovah's Witness, and besides, they pointed out that we were related.

But it was a distant relationship at best, third cousins once removed. I traced our family tree and discovered exactly how we were related. We had the same great-great grandparents, Francis Barclay and Agnes Beattie from Canonbie, Dumfries, Dumfriesshire, Scotland.

They had produced 10 children. One of their daughters, Elizabeth Barclay, was the matriarch of Ron's line. I came through their son, John Barclay.

I was 16 when Ron and I met, and that began a very hot and heavy relationship. Ron was 19. I missed him dearly through the week, when he was at college. He would visit me on the weekends.

Mostly we went to movies, but we also went to a semi-formal, which we dressed up for. Ron looked good in his suit, and I wore a white sparkly clingy dress, sleeveless, knee length with a scope neck. I remember he bought me a beautiful red rose corsage.

We were a very smart looking couple!

In 1967, when I was 17, we got the news that would change our lives. My mother had leukemia. The doctors expected her to live for another two years at most.

I have a pretty good idea what caused my mother's cancer. I used to help her occasionally at her job at Able Dry Cleaners.

One day, I was helping her attach tags onto garments when a huge chemical spill occurred.

I could not stand the strong smell, and knew we had to leave. My father pleaded with my mother to leave, and even her boss told her to go home. The chemicals were known to be dangerous.

But Mom would not leave her job. I am convinced to this day that those chemicals caused her illness. We later learned that those specific dry cleaning chemicals are known to cause cancer, specifically leukemia.

As usual, my parents never confided in me. I learned the devastating news by overhearing their conversation. On discovering the news, I immediately decided to drop out of school and get a job.

My first summer job was cleaning and caring for a family's young children. I worked there for two and a half months. They gave me a very good reference.

Then I got a position in the fall of 1967 at Ginn Publishing Company as an expediting clerk. I was there less than four months. After that, I worked briefly at a photography studio on Kingston Road, moving photographs into different chemicals. From there, I went on to work as a receptionist at a hearing aid centre in Eglinton Square.

At that time, Ron was working at Brunswick of Canada, a company that manufactured pool tables. He soon applied for and got a job at I.B.M. This paved the way for us to get married, or at least to be able to afford marriage.

On my 18th birthday, Ron took me out to shop for an engagement ring. It was white gold, with three tiny diamonds on each side of the main stone. The matching band was white with nine diamonds, three on each side and three in the centre.

Ron's band was white gold embossed. On our first anniversary, he bought me another wide band to match his.

He proposed to me in his car in the driveway of my parents' house at 74 Blakemore Blvd.

Of course, I said yes. We'd already been dating for two years. I was so excited when we went into the house to tell my parents. I even went next door to show my ring to our neighbour. I was ecstatic!

They were all happy for me, but insisted that in order for us to marry, Ron had to first study the scriptures, so we could be married in the Kingdom Hall of the Jehovah Witness church.

Ron agreed. He loved me, and said if that was what he had to do, he would do it.

I admit I felt hypocritical, since Ron and I had been having sex since I was 17. We'd avoided pregnancy by using the rhythm method. According to our religion, we were supposed to remain chaste and not have any marital relations. I didn't dare tell my parents.

I felt guilty, but the feeling didn't stop me. It did cause me to doubt myself and question my religion, and even my relationship with Ron. These are questions that have plagued people, especially those with firm religious beliefs, since the beginning.

Of course, many people argue you wouldn't buy a pair of shoes without trying them on. Shouldn't we want to make very sure we are sexually compatible with the person who will share our life?

~Chapter Four~

And so our engagement began. We went to Bible Studies together. Ron had to choose a JW member to stand as his best man. Likewise my matron of honour had to be from the faith. We chose a couple who were friends of mine for those positions, and a couple of my friends from Kingdom Hall to be my bridesmaids. Ron chose my brother, Ken, and one if his cousins to be groomsmen.

I found a wedding dress for $50 at a second-hand store in the Toronto Fashion District. The fabric was peau de soie and it had a long train. I wanted to use that train to alter the style of the dress to one I loved in the Bridal Magazine. The peau de soie gown in the magazine was far too expensive for me at $2000. A neighbour of mine was a seamstress, and said she could transform my $50 dress to the style I wanted.

I purchased strands of pearls to be sewn onto the gown and headdress, also tulle to turn the veil into a Cathedral style veil. My neighbour charged $50 for the work, so for a hundred dollars, I got my $2000 dress.

My hair was pulled back and I added a fall that was gathered and entwined at the back.

The resulting custom-made dress was beyond my wildest dreams. I found drop pearl earrings to wear and ordered a dozen deep red roses, white carnations and baby's breath for my bouquet. My look was complete!

I also found ready-made dresses for the bridesmaids and the matron of honour, and purchased velvet ribbons with daisies at the end of each ribbon, for the girls to wear in their hair. I had their satin shoes dyed to match and ordered yellow daisies for the bridesmaids' bouquets, and white daisies for the matron of honour. The matron wore butter yellow, and the bridesmaids wore long mint green gowns. Ron, the best man and the groomsmen wore black tuxedos and white carnations.

My neighbour made my mother's dress and jacket in mauve and I ordered deeper mauve variegated carnations for my mother to wear.

At first, I wanted my mother to wear rose or pink, but Ron's mother was wearing peach and I thought rose would clash. My mother had salt and pepper hair, and the mauve looked really good on her.

During our year-long engagement, we saved up for the wedding, and on June 14th, 1969 at 3pm we were married in the Kingdom Hall of Jehovah's Witnesses, which at the time was located at 459 Birchmount Road. The Kingdom Hall is no longer located there. The sun was shining. My Dad drove me to the Kingdom Hall and walked me down the aisle.

I was very nervous, and don't remember the service at all. I do recall I was glad when it was over.

Of the 100 people invited, 98 attended the ceremony. Afterward, we went to Cedarbrook Park for photographs, and then to the reception hall at Watt's Restaurant at Markham Road and Lawrence Avenue.

The day was a lot of fun. We enjoyed a beautiful chicken dinner. Ron's mother, Mina, made the wedding cake, fruit cake, and a friend of Ron's father, who was a baker, iced the cake for us. Our topper was two doves on a heart.

My going-away outfit was turquoise and white, with a matching turquoise jacket and a chiffon wrapped turban style hat. I had saved all year for the outfits we wore during the first two days of our marriage and our honeymoon.

Our guests all formed a circle and sang as we departed. We stayed at Inn on the Park for our wedding night. It was everything a young couple would expect, full of excitement, romance, intrigue and expectation for the future.

The next morning we started our honeymoon by driving through Georgia and Washington DC. We saw Arlington Cemetery, Virginia Beach, Williamsburg and Virginia before finally driving to Tampa, Florida, where Ron's father was living at the moment.

We went deep-sea fishing. It was very hot and I got a little sea-sick. I loved the smell of the sea air. Everything was new and exciting. We enjoyed our three weeks together.

We had planned to both work for a couple of years and save our money before starting a family. However, about two months after our wedding day we were visiting Ron's mother's home in Lefroy when I starting vomiting.

Ron's grandmother, Christina Mary (Sheppard) Kelly was there. She took one look at me and said, "I bet you're pregnant."

The doctor took blood tests and confirmed it.

Looking back, I think I had been nauseous or throwing up almost from our wedding day. With everything going on, I hadn't been thinking clearly, so I had no idea.

I was sick for the entire nine months of my pregnancy. At one point, Ron took me for dinner to Watt's Restaurant, where our reception had been held. I had veal parmesan and made it as far as the parking lot of our apartment before throwing it all up. I was far too sick to work, miserable every day. So I became a housewife in our apartment at 215 Markham Road, apartment 701.

I began to read about pregnancy and babies and that is how I filled my time.

I had no idea what to expect. I was 19 years old when my first child was born, and turned 20 when he was two months old.

~Chapter Five~

What I've been avoiding in these memories is a terrible loss I suffered at this time that should have been so happy.

When I was only 19, and had been married two and a half months, my mother died of leukemia.

The night before she died, I visited her at Scarborough General Hospital. My mother, Irene, was very swollen. She looked bad and was in a great deal of pain. The disease was in her bones.

I was very weak and tired myself. Ron took me home. As we were in the elevator returning to our apartment, I was talking about the baby and how much my mother would love it, when Ron turned to me and said, "Your mother is never going to live to see the baby."

I told him never to say that again. I was definitely in denial about my mother's chances of living.

Early the next morning, on August 24, 1969, my father called to tell me the news. I could not believe it.

My mother, Irene Hazel (Petch) Sharpe, was dead at 49, far too young! She would never live to see the grandchildren she would so have loved.

My mother had been the second eldest of four girls and two boys born in Edam, Saskatchewan. Her parents were Lloyd Hall Petch, born Flesherton, Ontario, and Edith Alma Tomlinson born in Nesbitt, Manitoba.

Lloyd was a farmer and Edith was a homemaker. I recall that Edith was very artistic. She hooked rugs and made beautiful quilts. Her home was decorated with the many delicate touches made by her own hands.

I still own the quilt Edith had made many years earlier for my mother, Irene.

Edith had long grey hair that she wore pinned up. I met her only once, when I was 14 years old. We had driven out west that summer, in 1964. I wrote to her constantly.

Lloyd, my grandfather, was a quiet man with a good sense of humour. He had been a quality horseman in his day, good at breeding and caring for his horses.

My mother's sister, Audrey, who has also since passed away, told me that my mother was also very artistic. However, Irene was a perfectionist who never kept any of her own work, believing it was not good enough. Irene also played the guitar as a young girl. I never saw any evidence of this artistic side of my own mother.

But I was aware of her perfectionism. It followed her into every part of our family life, from cleaning, to cooking, knitting and sewing and even in how she presented her children. It was her personal demon, perfectionism. She was never happy with anything she did, and never believed her efforts were good enough.

I believe my mother was an extremist. In one incident, she went on a starvation diet for a month. Then later, she ate a dozen donuts in one sitting. I don't know what that behaviour was about.

But my guess is that her extremism followed her into her religious life. In my opinion, her chosen religion, Jehovah's Witnesses, is an extremist faith. My mother's parents had also been Jehovah's Witnesses. They entered the religion the same way my mother did, by answering a knock on the door later in their lives.

Others of my family members also follow that faith, including my mother's youngest sister and her family, and a number of cousins.

I no longer have much in common with my extended family. Between the geographic distances, they are mostly located in Western Canada, and the religion, we have been largely separated.

My parents met during the Second World War, at the Palais Royale, a dance hall on the Toronto waterfront. Dad asked Mom to dance. They were married six months later, on December 20, 1941.

However, they did not have children immediately. I was born nine years later, in 1950. Irene was unable to carry pregnancies, and had three miscarriages before I was born, and another between my birth and my brother's.

Frustrated, my mother changed doctors before I was born. Her eldest sister Helen's doctor checked her over and put her on a regimen of vitamins and sensible eating. Soon after she began taking better care of herself, I came on the scene.

After my mother died, I became depressed, but didn't realize it. The day of her funeral, Dad warned me not to show my emotions in public. He said people would say I would not see my mother again if I cried. So I wept in my apartment, but not in public. I felt like a zombie. There was no happiness, only numbness, as if my life had ended.

My mother and I had been very close. I had called her every day when I was a teenager, working, as well as shortly before her death, when I was home. She could be difficult at times, but she was a good mother and always did the best she could. Her main flaw was that extremism I've already mentioned, and her failure to take good care of herself.

Her emotions and behaviour were unpredictable, up and down. This is a common trait in people with addiction issues or who had experienced abusive childhoods. I don't believe she was an addict, nor did she have an abusive childhood. But it is possible, looking back, that she may have been bipolar.

In later years, I came to realize her childhood had been anything but easy. Her family relied on her from a young age to earn money. She started working at the age of 16 to care for a household of five other brothers and sisters in Saskatchewan.

My mother never complained. That's not always a good thing. In my opinion, she didn't take the time to allow herself to feel or to satisfy her own needs. She always had too much on her plate, but never took the time to rest or care for herself. She believed that to do so would be selfish. She was a hard person to understand.

Her funeral was held at the same Kingdom Hall I had been married in. After the service, I never set foot in a Kingdom Hall again. I think it's telling that, once my mother was gone, I had no more connection to the faith.

On Friday night, in the middle of March, 1970, I suddenly felt a surge of energy. Spring was in the air. I remember walking around the block with a neighbour who was pregnant. Also, that night I felt I was about to go into labour. I called Ron. The doctor said when the pains were 20 minutes apart, Ron should drive me to the hospital.

It was a snowy night. I was in labour for 24 hours. The nurse wanted me to have a Caesarean section birth, but I refused. I felt I could deliver our baby naturally.

I sat up and started pushing, and at 7pm my first child was born. A healthy boy, 8 lbs and 7.5 oz., with black curly hair and blue eyes. He was 21 and a half inches long. I watched him enter the world!

I tried so hard to breast feed him, but to no avail. I had an infected nipple and both were inverted, so he wasn't getting any nourishment. I decided to feed him formula.

After 9 days old, he was still hungry after formula, so I started him on Pablum in the evening to help him sleep. By three months, he was sleeping through the night.

About three months after our first baby was born, I suffered a nervous breakdown. I was told it was post-natal depression. I was walking and pushing the baby carriage back and forth for hours on the corner of Eglinton Avenue and Markham Road, near our apartment building.

I believe someone called the police and they contacted my husband, who took me to the hospital.

Ron asked me what I'd been doing, and I told him I was walking the baby. I remember him taking me to Scarborough General, the Psychiatric Ward.

I'm not sure how long I was there, maybe one month, maybe three. I was kept full of drugs and I may have been treated with shock therapy, I'm not sure. All I know is it was awful.

Ron's mother, Mina, cared for our baby until I was able. Someone took photos of me during that time. I looked terrible. I wish they hadn't taken the photos.

I believe my marriage, followed so closely by my mother's death and the birth of our first child, had been simply too much for me. I'd been raised within what was, in my opinion, a cult, sheltered from the rest of the world and kept close to my mother. Losing her at such a critical time in my young married life had been a devastating blow.

My father was not able to adjust to life as a widower. He remarried on May 1, 1971, to a woman he'd known for only six months. Before he married Teivel, he asked me what I thought. I told him, in my opinion, it was too soon, and he should date other women before making a commitment.

Of course, he didn't listen to me. My father, Jack Telford Denis Sharpe, married Teivel (not her real name) in her home in Scarborough. They had a reception at Fran's Restaurant in Toronto.

I was pregnant with our second child at the time. I'd had a perm done at the hairdresser's for his wedding. It went very curly and frizzy, like a chrysanthemum. No one warned me that your body chemicals change when you are pregnant and that it will affect your hair's ability to take a perm.

I wore pink hot pants and a long jacket with a white blouse to the wedding. It was the only time I had photographs taken with our family together.

My father asked Ron to be his best man. Jack and Teivel went to Hawaii for their honeymoon. While they were gone, I took my single bedroom suite to my apartment for our first child to use. My father had given me permission to do that. Something told me to do it right away, while they were gone, or I might never have the chance.

I was right about that.

As soon as they returned from their honeymoon, Teivel began to make demands on my father. I asked for my mother's sewing machine, but was told Teivel planned to use it. She never did, but I never saw it again.

From the time they married, Teivel took over my father's life like a vulture. She used her mixed race against us, claiming we didn't like her because of her race. She was miserable, manipulative, calculating, angry, vindictive and controlling. She made it clear there was no room in our father's life for us. She also used her religion as an excuse to have nothing to do with us.

Years later, when I was caring for my aging father, I asked him how he and Teivel had met. He said they met at a party, and she went after him immediately. That didn't surprise me. He was a vulnerable new widower, and a very immature, naïve adult person. She latched onto him and didn't let go.

My younger brother, Ken, worked during the summer at Rock Garden Camp, from 1965 until 1971. He pumped gas for the boats and did odd jobs for our family friends at the Burthwick's. One day, while washing Ken's clothes, our Aunt Connie found marijuana in the pocket of his jeans. She told us about this in the summer of 1971.

We decided to confront him, and involved another family friend, who was a policeman. Also, our friends who owned the camp joined us in the intervention. We were all concerned about my brother, who was about 15 or 16 at the time. We wanted him to see how dangerous it was to use drugs.

That's when it all came pouring out. My young brother felt our father no longer cared about him, or what he was doing. He was too busy going to meetings and running after Teivel. Teivel had destroyed a number of my brother's vinyl records, and was being generally unkind to him. He was feeling alone and unloved since our mother had died.

Ken hadn't wanted to worry me, since I was married and had my own family, and my own troubles.

I was shaken, and very worried about my brother and his future. I didn't want him giving up on life or giving in to sorrow.

After we left Ken at the camp, I was so upset I threw up. Ron and I decided to ask Ken to come and live with us. We would ask my dad to help financially, since we were a young couple with a baby and couldn't afford to add to our grocery budget.

I called my father to explain the situation and let him know we wanted Ken to live with us. When we spoke to Ken about it, he was elated at the prospect.

My father refused to pay for Ken's food, saying he could not afford it. He would have to sell Ken's life insurance policy to come up with food money for Ken.

I was so upset with my father! He had the money. I was trying to make sure my brother completed high school, while my father seemed to be trying to get Ken to quit school.

When Ken came to live with us, it was in our two-bedroom apartment in Markham. There were four of us, Ron and me, my brother Ken, our toddler and another baby on the way. It was tight, but we managed. Isn't that what families are supposed to do?

Ken had a friend who lived in Markham who picked him up and drove him to and from school every day. He slept in the same room as our toddler, while I was pregnant with our second child. He lived with us a total of six years.

After Ken finished high school, Ron asked him what his plans were. Ken said he was thinking of traveling around Europe. Ron expected Ken to get a job, and told him if he wasn't planning on finding employment, he couldn't continue to live with us. So Ken found a job working at a factory.

Eventually, Ken went to work for his friend, whose father had a landscaping company. Ken took a course to increase his skills, then applied to the City of Toronto for a job as a labourer. He was hired and worked for the city for about 30 years, succeeding and working his way into the management team. He retired in 2011.

Who knows what might have happened to him if we had not taken him into our home? I'm extremely grateful for the way his life worked out.

My father was hardly around while we were raising our children. My mother was dead, so they had no grandmother, and in my opinion, my father had no excuse. Our children had no grandfather, either, really.

My father missed out on a lot, but so did we. There is not much more I can say about it, other than that I feel a loss that is beyond my understanding. Even now, if I think about those days, with no help or support from my father and trying to come to grips with the loss of my mother, I can easily slip into utter despair, not only for my own sake, but for the whole family.

I do my best not to dwell on the past.

~Chapter Six~

Our second son was born in 1972, with fair hair and blue eyes, weighing 7 lbs, 6 ½ oz. Because our specialist was planning to be away, my labour was induced. They started the drip at 9 am, and by 2:34 pm our son came into the world. It was a very easy delivery.

Unlike with our first child, I had not gained a lot of weight. As a result, it was a very easy birth and he was a relaxed, easy-going baby from the start. I didn't torture myself trying to breastfeed. Instead, our second was on formula from the start, and slept well through the night.

However, I had another post-natal breakdown, approximately six months after giving birth. The episode was very severe, to the point where I didn't recognize my own children. The breakdown happened very suddenly, overnight. I was taken to the hospital and had to stay there quite a while, clouded by excessive drugs.

During my stay in the hospital, my maternal grandmother, Edith Alda (Tomlinson) Petch, died on April 24, 1973, in Turtleford, Saskatchewan. I wasn't aware at the time of her death.

Sometime later, while we were vacationing at a rented cottage, I wondered aloud why I hadn't heard from my grandmother. Ron then told me about her death.

I was in shock, both over her death and over the fact no one had seen fit to tell me. I was never given the option to attend her funeral or to say a proper good-bye. It was a terrible feeling of loss.

On top of that, she had left me a small sum of money, $625. Without discussing it with me, Ron had decided to use that money for a new motor for our Volkswagen Beetle.

I had no doubt we needed the motor, and it probably was the best use of the money at the time.

But I was starting to see a pattern, one where decisions were being consistently made for me, without my consent or contribution.

I remember feeling honoured that my grandmother had thought to leave this money to my brother and me, since our mother had already passed on, but that feeling was overshadowed by the disappointment of having no say in how the money was to be used.

Life does have its share of disappointment!

After recovering from my second breakdown, my time was spent raising our children and organizing our home.

We'd purchased our first home when I was eight months pregnant with our second child. When we went to apply to purchase our home in Malvern, there was a little trailer on the corner of Sheppard and Lapsley. It was crowded with so many people that I had to push my way through. People could see I was pregnant and they were sympathetic. I was able to get close enough to get a lot.

If we'd politely stayed at the back of the crowd, we would not have been able to obtain a lot to purchase. So I was glad I'd had the nerve to push myself forward.

Of course, our moving date was delayed, as these things always are with new homes. We were supposed to move in before our second child was born, but it was actually the late fall after his birth when we finally took possession.

The new house seemed huge, after living in a two-bedroom apartment with my brother and our two small children. I remember saying to Ron, "How will we ever fill it?"

All of my time was spent caring for our two children and our home. Believe me it didn't take long to fill the space. My husband Ron worked hard for I.B.M. right up till his retirement, so we never had to worry about paying bills or putting food on the table in those years. In fact, we were able to pay off our mortgage in just five years, by having automatic payments made for IBM stock each pay day. You don't miss what you don't have to spend.

Ron was always dependable, a good provider who put his family first. He had his hobbies: fishing, hockey, baseball, going to the cottage we rented. Generally, he was a home boy, who escaped the stress of a difficult job by spending time in his home with his family.

We both loved to travel, and that was something we enjoyed very much as a family.

If he had one flaw, it was drinking. As our marriage deteriorated, Ron's drinking increased. He seemed incapable of communicating to me what was bothering him, instead drinking more and more.

Our problems might have been resolved, if only he could have talked with our marriage counsellor, but we'll never know.

I know it's also my fault. I should have told him how much I appreciated all the things he did as a husband and father, how dependable and caring he had always been. I have my own regrets, but I know I did the best I could at the time. To this day I still love him and think he was a great guy.

But Ron would simply not talk to me, and I couldn't stay. I felt I had no choice. Communication was a problem for me as well as for Ron, but of course I didn't see that at the time. I was full of the idea that I was right and he was wrong, and I would not listen to my psychologist or anyone else.

I take my share of the blame, after all is said and done.

Here's the question I should have asked myself: Do you want to be right, or be happy?

Keep that question in mind when life presents you with difficult choices.

I wish I'd had the sense to think of it at the time.

In 1974, I was feeling bored. I decided to take a night school class in Elementary Oil Painting at Cedarbrae High School. I received a certificate.

Taking those classes filled my time and made my life more interesting.

For the next five years, I continued to take night school classes. My next course was Life Drawing, which embarrassed me because I didn't realize the models would be nude.

In 1977-78 I studied Interior Design 1, followed by an Introduction to Psychology. Then in 1980 I studied making stained glass with a friend. My final course, in 1980-81, was Basic Brush Strokes – Advanced Techniques in Ceramics. I received a certificate in this course after taking a ceramic class.

This began my love for ceramics and I became a ceramic artist. It was obvious I had a craving to learn, especially in the arts.

I'd often wondered whether my paternal grandfather, Telford Wright Sharpe was still alive. My paternal grandparents had separated and divorced when my father was a baby. My father's sister, Evelyn Arloah Sharpe, had been only a year older than him when she went to live with her father. However, it seems that Telford's parents actually raised his daughter, Evelyn. She lived with her grandparents Matthew Gray Sharpe and Mary Ella Ellen

(Wright) Sharpe. Her father, Telford Wright Sharpe, lived in the house next door.

In or around 1974, my mother-in-law, Mina (Constable) Kelly, informed me she had found an article in the newspaper saying that my grandfather, Telford Wright Sharpe, was in a nursing home in Brantford. His High School class was having a reunion. This proved my grandfather was still alive.

From the time his father left, taking his sister, my father had never had any contact with them. He'd never even seen a photo of them. So when his sister, Evelyn, died on June 21, 1932 at the age of 15, he had no knowledge of it. She died of sarcoma of the ovary, a rare form of ovarian cancer.

Too many secrets followed my father's family. When his sister died, he never knew, or attended the funeral. On top of that, he was told she'd died in a tobogganing accident, having broken her neck. Jack's mother also never attended her daughter's funeral, and had no contact with her after her husband left her for her grandparents to raise.

A strange set of family circumstances. All parties are now buried in Mount Hope Cemetery in Brantford.

If my mother-in-law had not found the newspaper clipping, I would not have known that my grandfather was still alive. It was about 1974 when I decided to call the nursing home and try to speak with him. When I reached him, he said he would be glad to meet me and my family.

My husband, Ronald, drove all of us, myself, our children and my brother Ken and his girlfriend to the nursing home.

I had researched the Sharpe family and learned that my grandfather, Telford's paternal grandparents were

John Sharpe and Ellen Gray. They both came from Sligo, Ireland with their parents in approximately 1836, and landed in Rawdon Twsp., Malcom, Quebec, where they met and married on July 18, 1842. Their marriage date was slightly different according to a 1988 Census, which indicated they'd married in 1843, and moved to Innisfil, in South Simcoe, Ontario.

They lived in Innisfil all their married lives and raised 12 children.

John Sharpe and Ellen Gray were among the earliest settlers in Innisfil. They are buried in Thornton Union Cemetery in Essa, Ontario with some of their children.

A photograph of the whole family was taken in 1878 and was given to the Simcoe Archives by their son Scott Sharpe. That's where I found the photo.

My great grandfather, Matthew Gray Sharpe, was in the photograph.

I found the research amazing, but when I asked my Dad if he wanted to meet his father, he said, "No."

Telford Wright Sharpe was a small man. He wore glasses and a sweater over a flannel shirt. He seemed very mild, and told us he had diabetes. As a younger man, he had played in a band and was a builder of sorts.

I later found out he'd been a jack-of-all-trades. He seemed pleasant enough, but what can you really tell from a short meeting with an elderly man?

I took some photos of that day of our family meeting with Telford. I included Telford's photo in my book of three generations. I had no idea how close he was to dying at the time.

Two weeks later, my Dad called to say he wanted to meet Telford after all. We arranged a time when I would be able to make the trip with my father and his wife, Teivel.

Dad drove, and we barely spoke in the car. I really didn't get along with Teivel, as I mentioned earlier.

I introduced my father, Jack Telford Denis Sharpe, to his father Telford Wright Sharpe. It was late fall, 1976. We had a pleasant enough meeting, and I was glad to help the two finally come into contact. They had never had any knowledge of each other.

However, at some point, inevitably, my father and Teivel brought out the JW literature and gave Telford the *Awake* and *Watchtower* magazines to read. It was uncomfortable, to say the least. I believe grandfather Telford was a Baptist. I have no way of knowing what he thought of all the JW talk.

The meeting ended shortly after the JW literature came out. I never saw my grandfather again.

Telford died on November 16, 1976.

After this meeting with Telford, I'd asked my father and Teivel not to say anything to my Great Aunt Margaret. I didn't know what reaction I'd get from Aunt Margaret, because she'd never had a positive thing to say about Telford, and I'd only ever heard negative stories about my grandfather.

I worried that if she learned about our visit, she might be hurt.

Then one day when I was speaking to Aunt Margaret, she asked me about my grandfather Telford Sharpe. "What did you think of him?" she asked. "How did the visit go?"

I was dumbfounded and it took me a moment before I asked her how she'd learned about our meeting.

"Oh," she answered, "Teivel told me."

I was really angry and told Aunt Margaret I'd asked Teivel and my father not to say anything. "I think Teivel only told you about it to cause trouble," I said.

"I think so too," Aunt Margaret agreed.

However, Aunt Margaret understood why I would want to meet my grandfather and thought it was wonderful that I'd reconnected him with my father. So, Teivel's plan to cause trouble backfired. She was always on the lookout for a chance to cause rifts in the family, in hopes all inheritances would go to my father, and in turn to her.

My father's unusual childhood, with no contact with his father or sister, helps me to explain a lot of things I didn't understand when I was younger. He had always been easily led by my mother, and manipulated by his second wife who used their religion as a crutch. It explained why he seemed so childlike, and could not seem to think for himself. He was easy prey, and didn't have a chance.

For this reason, among others, I was able to forgive Dad and rise above the hurt caused by the way he had shunned my brother and myself and our families. I'm not condoning the way he turned his back on us in favour of his second wife and his religion. I'm just trying to make sense out of it all.

Ken and I had always at least had a cordial relationship with our father before Teivel came on the scene. Once they were married, they tried to have as little to do with us as possible, and the feeling was mutual. She was simply too unpleasant. I always thought of her as "Teivel the gold digger". Her main ambition seemed to be to clean my father out of his money.

I learned about my grandfather's death when a Christmas card was returned to me marked "deceased". I immediately called my father to let him know. He surprised me by saying he already knew, and had received a small inheritance of $9,000.

I was very hurt and angry that my father had known since November and hadn't told me about my grandfather passing. After all, I was the one who had brought them together.

When I told him how I felt, Jack said, "I didn't think about that."

To this day, I am still hurt by the fact that my father never thought to tell me when my grandfather died. I'm sure I can see Teivel's hand in that. After all, I was the instrument that allowed him to make peace with his father while he was still alive. I was the one who cared enough to do the research and to track him down and to encourage my father to go with us to see him.

In my opinion, that kind of thoughtlessness is not very Christian in nature.

In my eyes, both Teivel and my father seemed very selfish, self-absorbed and completely wrapped up in their own lives and their cult religion. Between the Jehovah's Witnesses and Teivel's family, there was no time or energy left for my father's family.

Due to my father's shunning, I felt neglected, unloved, hurt, ashamed and alone, like someone with a contagious disease. I remember I used to call my father on the phone, but our conversations were always cut short by Teivel in the background making some demand. He always chose to give in to her and cut our conversation short. That was how it went for the entire 37 years that my father was married to Teivel.

Eventually, I came to the conclusion there was no point in calling. I was tired of being told there was no time for me or my family, of being stepped on. It also made me angry to see Dad not stick up for himself.

I still have tears in my eyes while writing these pages. Even though my father is gone from this earth, the scars of his neglect remain deep in my soul even after all this time. I hope this helps my readers understand how hurt I was, and no amount of money can ever erase that pain.

All I ever wanted was for my father to be a Dad to me, and to help me cope with the loss of my mother in the way a parent should. That's why I started writing this memoir, as a kind of therapy to release these emotions. It's not healthy to harbour anger, pain, sorrow, regret. It only keeps you down. I want to move forward, because we cannot change the past.

After my grandfather, Telford, died, a strange thing occurred. In his will, he referred to his son as a friend, and not as a son, which makes me think he did not believe he was really my father's father. I remember my father was deeply offended that his wording said "friend" instead of "son". I have no way of knowing for sure what the old man meant, whether he really doubted he was the father, and maybe that's what caused him to leave my grandmother and father and return with his daughter to his parent's home.

Of course, I can't ask him, and this is only my speculation. But I wanted to include this, because my family had so many strange secrets, that we'll never be able to resolve.

I started babysitting in the fall of 1976, when a neighbour asked me to look after her son. This gave me the money to purchase my dining room suite and a chesterfield and chair, which we needed desperately. Our furniture was beginning to wear thin.

This neighbour also introduced me to the Malvern Presbyterian Church, and the minister, his wife and family, got me involved in the church.

I continued with my in-home daycare for about two years, from 1976-1978, until I was about 28 years old. At that time, my youngest son was starting full time school.

The reason I stopped my daycare was that it was beginning to cause me a lot of anxiety. I was caring at the time for a young baby, and I started having dreams that something bad would happen to him and I would not be able to save him.

The responsibility was wearing me out and Ron agreed I should give it up.

In August of 1976 I earned a certification to be an instructor for The Diet Workshop. I had completed the course to instruct members and had also personally lost weight. I held a lifetime membership.

I remember I spoke at one class and hated the experience of addressing the group. It gave me the feeling that I was pretending to know everything, and I knew how little I really knew. So I resigned from that as well.

At around the same time, something very strange happened that I was in no way prepared to handle.

Through my involvement with The Diet Workshop, I had met a lady who shared my interest in antiques. Both she and her husband enjoyed antiques, as did Ron and I.

Because they didn't drive, Ron and I would pick them up and we would head out to maybe see a movie and walk around Ontario Place.

After looking at the shops, we went for dinner.

We made an early evening of it. After we dropped them off, I confided to Ron that my friend's husband had been continually putting his hand on my thigh and I'd had to continually remove it.

Ron proceeded to tell me that the wife, my so-called friend, had been doing the same thing to him!

We were both mortified and the whole idea made our skin crawl. We agreed we would not see them again. The next day, this lady had the audacity to call me. I told her we could not be friends, and Ron and I were not into swapping partners.

That was the last I ever heard from either of them.

Also around this time, I volunteered with the Scouts and Beavers because I thought it would be good for my sons. I ended up being voted to be the Scouting Auxiliary President, which meant I was involved in apple day, organizing the father and son banquet and organizing a Christmas play.

I guess I was given more responsibility than I'd bargained for. I continued in the role for a year.

Then my eldest son informed me he no longer wanted to be a Scout, so that ended that, and our younger son followed suit. To replace the activity, Ron got them involved in skating and hockey, and that kept them busy. It was really Ron's bag, doing those things. I went along to support the boys. Our eldest stuck with it, but our younger son soon lost interest.

In the spring of 1977, my brother Ken became engaged to the young woman he'd been dating for around two years. They were engaged for about a year, saving up to get married. I threw a shower for her, as did her sister and a friend, so she did pretty well in the gift department. We held the wedding rehearsal in our home in 1978. I had everything decorated for St. Patrick's Day. We had a white linen tablecloth and a centerpiece of white carnations sprayed green. We had clover shortbread cookies and mint chocolate chip ice cream for dessert, all green in honour of St. Patrick's Day.

I was to be the bridesmaid.

My father started making noises about not attending the wedding, because Teivel didn't feel comfortable since her children were not invited.

My brother didn't even know her children. He had no relationship with them at all.

I remember telling my father, Jack, on the phone, "You are Ken's father. If Teivel isn't comfortable she can stay home, but you need to go because you are Ken's Dad." I said that I bet if he told Teivel he was going no matter what, she would give in and agree to go as well.

And that's exactly what happened. He said he would come, and Teivel came with him.

Ken was married in 1978 in a large wedding at Christ Anglican Church in Toronto. The reception was at Fantasy Farms Banquet Hall, the Cinderella Room.

We wanted our sons to see Ken get married because he had lived with us since they were born. He was more like a brother to them than an uncle. It took a lot of arranging. Uncle Max and Aunt Connie took the boys to the church, and then our neighbour took them home afterward. Ron gave them money for pizza since we planned to be at the reception till quite late. They spent the night at our neighbour's house.

It would have been much easier for us if the boys could have stayed for the reception, but the bride and groom wanted only adults at the reception, and so we worked it out so everyone was happy.

I admit, I had become very attached to having my brother around. When he married and moved out, I was very upset and missed him a lot.

Shortly after they were married, Ken and his wife invited our family over for dinner. Through the entire evening they badgered our children to sit still and to not touch things. By the time the evening was over, I was furious at my brother, and ready to let go of missing him so much!

This was a side of my brother I'd never seen before, and I didn't like it at all. That evening was very important to me; it got me over the hurdle of loneliness and depression at missing Ken. Maybe that's what it was supposed to do!

Anyway, I didn't look back. My brother had gone on with his life, which was the right thing to do and I did the same.

My brother and his wife had three children. Their first daughter was born in 1980, their second daughter in 1983. My brother helped to deliver her in the car on the way to the hospital, and their story appeared in the local newspaper. After that, we called him Dr. Red, because of his red hair.

Their third child, a son, was born in 1987.

I've been around for all of the births and have done a lot of babysitting over the years. The whole family has turned out to be really great people. My eldest niece works as a child care therapist. Her sister is a communications director and their baby brother now works as a paramedic. So they all turned out very well, and I'm so proud of them all!

In June of 1980 I joined Malvern Presbyterian Church and volunteered as a group leader. I was trying to give my children some kind of faith, or at least enough knowledge to offer them a choice of what to believe. At the time, it seemed to be a good idea. I had never been christened, so I was christened into the church.

I guess I was looking for something, but who knows what. To this day, I still don't know if joining the church was the right thing to do. All any of us can do is the best we can.

I never had my own children christened, and to this day they are not. I wanted them to have a choice, which was something I never had. They have never felt it was necessary to be christened.

In October of 1980, boredom once again got the better of me and I began working in ceramics. I took about two classes, and after that began designing and glazing my own custom items to coordinate rooms and custom work. I became passionate about hand-painting, glazing and creating all different kinds of pieces. You could say I was obsessed. Ron bought me a kiln that Christmas of 1980 and I was totally in shock! I never expected such an expensive and thoughtful gift. It was probably the best Christmas gift I've ever received.

I started creating custom pieces on consignment. I sold pieces at the Caddy Shack in Perry Sound. It worked out well. I became a true ceramic artist. To this day, I could probably pick up a green ware piece, clean it, fire it and paint it, then fire and glaze it, just like I'd never left off.

Like riding a bike.

At some point, I teamed up with my neighbour, the same one who had introduced me to the Malvern church. We tried to start a business together. We had a party at my house and took a lot of orders, including a lot of custom orders.

We planned to call the business S&S Ceramics, because her maiden name started with S and so did mine.

Unfortunately, it turned out that I was doing 90% of the work and I resented that, so the business fell apart.

In the spring of 1980, on May 9, my mother-in-law Mina Janet Kelly died suddenly of a heart attack in her home in Lefroy. It was a devastating shock for both me and my husband, Ron, Mina's only child.

About a month later, in June, Ron's cousin also died in a car accident at the age of 30. She had been full of life and to this day she is sadly missed.

~Chapter Seven~

I'd been working at the YMCA for about a year, and was also saving money from my child care work. I babysat children and did arts and crafts with them. My goal was to save enough money for a trip to the Bahamas. My neighbour, the one who wanted to enter a business with me, and I had booked the trip. It was to take place for a week, shortly after Mina had passed away.

I felt bad about leaving Ron so soon after his mother passed. I offered to cancel the trip and stay with him, but he said it was already paid for, and there was nothing else I could do, so I should go.

I still had reservations, but what Ron said made sense. The trip was paid for, and there was nothing else I could do. So off I went with my neighbour to the Bahamas for a week.

It turned out to be a total disaster. I got sick on the first night from brushing my teeth with tap water. While I was in bed, my friend got involved in a sexual affair with a man she had just met. She was a married woman with two children at home. The only reason I knew what she was up to is that she came back to the room to check on me and told me.

I was too sick to climb out of bed. Also, I was in shock at what this friend was doing, and she was an elder in the church as well. When I was finally feeling well enough to leave the room, some old businessman invited us to his room for drinks. I was very uncomfortable and so we left after a short time.

I met a young man who invited me to dance, and I agreed. There was a definite attraction between us. He walked me to my room, kissed me on the cheek and left. I had spent most of the evening talking about my husband and children. At some point he asked me if I was so happy, why was I there with him?

When I thought about his question later, I wasn't able to come up with an answer. That really bothered me. The only reply I could muster was that I was on vacation and he'd asked me to dance, end of story.

This man was not a coast guard, but had arrived on his own boat. I had decided I would not see him again, but for some reason I made the mistake of not immediately cutting the ties.

I hadn't had enough sleep during our stay and was drinking far too much, something I wasn't at all used to. That's no excuse, but it may explain why I was making so many crazy decisions.

I was somehow able to get in touch with the coast guard, who told me he was returning to Florida where his four children lived. We arranged that he would be able to contact me at my neighbour's house.

It was all very exciting, and romantic, making plans while we were on vacation in the Bahamas. However, back at home, it was not pleasant at all!

I felt very guilty and mixed up for what had happened on that vacation, also I felt over-tired and out of focus. I couldn't sleep. I didn't know what to do or who to talk to about it all.

At the time, I decided to confide in our minister. I'd actually admitted the whole thing to Ron because I felt so guilty about it. We'd always been honest with each other, and I felt that was the best thing to do.

I'd like to make it very clear that I never did sleep with this man, but even though it never went that far, I still felt I'd betrayed my husband. I had no experience with romance, having married Ron very young. I truly had never had anyone to talk to about these things.

I couldn't talk to Ron about it as he was hurting. The tension in our home was unbearable. My neighbour offered to let me stay at her place for a few days. She was trying to convince me that I should leave Ron, take our kids and go to live with the stranger I'd just met.

I knew that would never happen, but I was thoroughly confused. No one other than Ron had ever shown interest in me, and I was caught up in the romance of it.

While I was in this state of turmoil and confusion, I made the mistake of contacting the man.

I told our minister the whole story, about my neighbour's affair in the Bahamas, about the young man and being still in touch with him, about how terrible the tension was in our home. He wanted to help Ron and me smooth things out and get back to being happy together. He made up a set of rules for us to follow. He became our communicator.

The next time the man called me from Florida, I told him I would not leave my husband and children and that he had to stop calling me. He called me a bitch and then hung up on me. So, he was a real sweetie! I felt like such a fool to have believed and fallen for his bullshit.

At least I had cut it off completely, ended it. It had been nothing more than a meaningless flirtation but had caused a great deal of trouble.

In addition to the minister's rules for me in making amends with Ron, Ron also had a couple of rules and I agreed with them.

First, he insisted I end the friendship with the young man entirely. I did that. Second, he wanted me to end the friendship and business ties with my neighbour, as he believed she was a bad influence on me. I agreed and ended that as well.

So I called my neighbour and ended that friendship and business venture. That was a blessing in disguise as she had not been helping me at all.

Except even after all that was done, I still could not sleep. My mind started racing through everything that had happened. It was very upsetting. I could not seem to calm down the hornet's nest in my mind.

Uncle Max asked me to visit him in Perry Sound. He thought a visit to the country might help me. I don't remember whether it was me or Ron who had called him. So I went north for a few days, but it didn't help.

When I got back home, things were even worse. I ended up in Whitby Psychiatric Hospital, and it was like a scene from *One Flew Over the Cuckoo's Nest*. Years later they improved the look of the Whitby Hospital, but at the time it looked exactly like in that movie.

The psychiatrist put me on an experimental drug called Modicate. It was intended to slow the mind down. It had the effect of shutting my whole body down. For a year I didn't have a period and I couldn't talk. I wasn't eating much either.

I don't know how long I was in the hospital. I do recall I was home for my second niece's birth, in June of 1983. The years surrounding that time are very fuzzy. I remember phoning Ron from the hospital and begging him to let me come home. I was also home for the birth of my eldest niece in November of 1980. The entire period is a haze. I believe I must have been home on weekends first, before coming home full time.

I know I was on the Modicate for at least a year. Meanwhile, Ron was looking after two young boys, a home, and working full time. He had no time to look after me, so it was probably a lot easier for him with me in the hospital.

He told me I'd have to participate in the activities in the hospital, put my name on the board, before they would let me come home. I had to prove I was able to do things.

So I played basketball, went swimming, went for walks, did exercises and breathing and listened to music. I think I was probably meditating. I did crafts and eventually I was allowed to return home.

Ron went to a marriage counsellor a couple of times, and I also went separately. I asked the counsellor, who was also my psychiatrist, to take me off the Modicate. He said he would see what could be done.

He told me I'd have to be weaned off it very slowly, as it was a powerful drug. You could not just stop taking it. So I agreed. He arranged for my family doctor to give me an injection once a month and weaned me off of it. The entire time I was on that drug, I didn't have a period. Also, it caused a terrible case of acne, especially as it was coming out of my system.

It also caused me to be very stiff and unable to move. It felt like the movie *Awakenings*. I felt imprisoned in my own body and not able to communicate.

When I came home, Ron told me I would have to rely on him going forward. He told me I'd have to listen only to him and not to other people, as they could not be trusted and I was too naïve to handle what they said.

In other words, it was a big bad world out there, and it would be best for me to stay at home and be a wife and mother and not get involved in outside interests, business, or study courses. He said if I just listened to him, everything would be fine.

He also said I had to get strong and better for our kids. He said, "Don't you want to live?" I said I wasn't sure.

Ron hugged me and said "Of course you do. It's just going to take time to get your strength back."

I asked him if he still loved me. He said of course he did, he wouldn't be there if he didn't.

I remember feeling as though he no longer needed me. He had a cleaning lady who came in. I asked him to cancel her so I could feel useful again and it would help me get my strength back.

When I starting housecleaning again, I felt terribly weak. It had been so long since I'd done anything. I wondered whether I would ever get better. And I looked a sight! The medication had caused huge red pimples all over my face.

I had the feeling of total incompetence from having messed up so badly, and from having spent time in Whitby Psychiatric Ward. I felt utterly lost, without any vitality. And I looked as awful as I felt.

The only thing that seemed to help was that Ron seemed to be rooting for me to get out of the doldrums. He still loved me. It gave me a purpose to work hard and resume my responsibilities.

However, Ron did arrange for me to visit a neighbour across the street every day, to spend time and have coffee with her. Her name was Betty. She was kind, four feet, ten inches tall and about 98 lbs. She was a heavy smoker but one of the nicest people. She made me feel welcome.

I remember telling Betty I wasn't going to get better and she said she didn't want to hear any more talk like that. She said it was just going to take time. She was someone I could vent to and I could also help her with her in-home daycare, looking after children. I also washed dishes and whatever she needed help with.

She gave me a purpose to my life, helped me to heal and feel whole again.

Unfortunately, she was living in a marriage that had once been very abusive. Her husband was a reformed alcoholic. He was no longer drinking but had once been a heavy drinker and she told me a number of stories in confidence, which I won't share.

By this point in their marriage, he was sober and was very kind, always willing to take her or the children anyplace they needed to go. I was there for the ride, so to speak, and they often took me out with them. I was thankful for the trips and the time I spent with them.

I didn't know what to expect from Betty and her husband. As the years have gone by, I've learned a lot more about the disease of alcoholism, which has unfortunately effected my own family.

I now realize that people with addictions are often two different people. They are one way when sober, and another when they are using.

I've learned they are usually not bad people, they just have a disease that is beyond their control.

One Christmas, Betty, her daughter and I took a bus to Scarborough Town Centre to go Christmas shopping. On the way, the snow started falling, picture perfect like a post-card. The entire bus load of people broke out suddenly singing Christmas Carols.

Nothing as beautiful as that had ever happened to me before, and it probably never would again. That was a time when people truly appreciated tradition and family. The older I get, the more I realize how perfect that evening was. I miss those times!

One Christmas Eve, Betty and her family spent the evening at our home.

At some point, I had to stop going over to Betty's so often, as I had to take care of my own family. Although we spent less time together, I've never forgotten Betty, or how she'd helped me, more than she would ever know.

Years later, her daughter called to tell me Betty had passed away. That was February 14, 2000, many years later.

Betty, I still miss you and think of you often!

In the spring of 1983, my father retired from his job as a postal clerk, after 37 years. He called to let me know. I suggested that he should pick me up and I'd take him out for a congratulatory drink. He agreed.

Dad had to stop at the store for something. While we were in line, he mentioned that he was worried about Teivel and the new watch he'd been given by Canada Post for his service.

I asked him why he was worried.

He said that he never knew what kind of mood she would be in, or how she would act. I offered to let him leave the watch at my place, and suggested that he not tell her. That way it would be safe and he wouldn't have to worry about it.

He thought that was a good idea. Then he dropped me off and went home.

A few hours later, there was a knock at my door. It was my father and Teivel.

Dad asked me to give him his watch back.

I said to Teivel, "You're not planning to throw it out, are you?"

She answered that she would do whatever she wanted with it.

I asked my father if he really wanted me to give it to her. He said yes, give it to her.

Later that evening, I called my father to ask what Teivel planned to do with the watch.

He told me she wanted him to give back the watch, as well as another gift, a knife, to the Post Office. She was jealous because when she'd left the Post Office, they hadn't given her anything.

I pleaded with him not to do that, telling him it would be an insult to his employer and his staff. They wanted him to have it for his service, that's why they gave it to him.

Of course, as always, he did what Teivel demanded. She bought him a replacement watch, but it wasn't as nice, was much cheaper, and besides didn't have the meaning for him that his retirement gift held. How could it mean the same?

What a demeaning thing for a wife to demand of her husband! Why he did it I will never understand. I consider that to be a form of spousal abuse, to force him to humiliate himself that way and to insult his friends and colleagues of many years, people who obviously respected and loved him.

~Chapter Eight~

In the summer of 1983 my Great Aunt Margaret called to tell me she was very weak and had a terrible rash. Her doctor had told her to put Vaseline on it, but it was getting worse and she was almost fainting.

I called my father and asked him to fetch Margaret and bring her to my house, since I didn't drive.

When she arrived, I could see how weak she was. I called my family doctor, whose practice was across the street, and asked him to come over and see her.

He wasn't happy about the house call, they don't do that anymore, but he came. He could see immediately that she had shingles and gave me a prescription for a salve and some powder that you use in water to soak cloths, then apply the wet fabric to her body where the rash was visible. Then he ordered her to get some rest.

Soon she was feeling much better, and was very grateful to me for looking after her and helping her return to normal.

I could see she was still frail from age, and offered to let her move into my house so I could look after her. But she declined the offer. She never wanted to be a burden to anyone.

"You have your own life," she said.

Once she was well enough, I decided to hold an 87th birthday party for her at our home. It would be the end of August. I invited her cousins and my aunt and uncles for dinner to celebrate her birthday, which was to be on September 3. I had a beautiful cake made especially for her, and I know she loved it. I'm so glad I had the chance to do that for her!

Not long after Margaret returned to her home, she called to say she was putting her house and cottage up for sale. I asked her if she'd like me to help her get ready to sell the places. She said she would appreciate the help, so that's how I came to be involved in helping her find a retirement home.

It was too big a decision for Margaret to contend with alone. She had narrowed the choice down to three places. I don't know how we made the decision, but somehow we did.

Before moving into a retirement and nursing home, there are a lot of preliminary steps. At the time, I didn't have my driver's license, so we had to take taxis to all of her appointments. I would take the bus to her place, and from there she would pay for a taxi to her appointments and I would accompany her.

Somehow we got everything done, but between the appointments and helping her clean the home she'd lived in for 41 years, it was a lot! It really took a toll on me.

It was a lot of work going through everything to see what was important, and what could be thrown out. The first thing I remember was searching for her diamond rings. She told me they had been lost for a long time, and she could not find them.

I did eventually find them. They were in a six quart basket full of rusted old tools and junk, in a cotton bag in her bedroom. She did not remember putting them there.

I also found two handguns under her bed. One had a pearl handle with a lot of filigree work embossed on it. The other was just a plain steel gun. I loved the pearl handled gun, but what could I do with it, other than admire it?

When I showed them to her, she said she had forgotten all about them. She said they belonged to her brother-in-law, James Clarkson Spring. How she ended up with them, I'll never know. I don't think she even remembered.

I planned to bring them home on the subway, but when I called Ron, he said not to. It was illegal to carry hand guns in Canada without a license. He said to hide them somewhere in the house, and he would later give them to the police.

So I hid them in a box of maxi pads in the washing machine in her basement.

It must have taken about a year to clear out Aunt Margaret's house. By the summer of 1984 we had a trip planned to go to the west coast. We got Aunt Margaret settled in the senior home, Chester Village at 717 Broadview Avenue. It was run by the United Church, near the home she was leaving.

As Ron and I drove her to the home, she was incoherent, as if the ordeal was just too much for her. I think she must have been mentally denying where we were going.

I remember the garage was full. We gave half of the belongings to the Goodwill and the other half to the Salvation Army. Ken and I took whatever furnishings and things we could to remember her by, but the rest we just couldn't keep.

My brother, Ken, arranged for the police to come by the house and turned the handguns over to them while we were out west on our trip.

As soon as we got Aunt Margaret settled into her new place, I was just returning home on the bus and arrived to find Ron talking with Margaret on the phone. I recall Ron saying to her that I'd gone to a lot of trouble and she would have to be patient and try to make the adjustment.

She insisted on speaking to me. I took the phone and she started to complain about the place. She didn't like it and wanted me to find her someplace else to live.

I told her she would have to give it a chance. We had our trip already booked and I couldn't do anything more. I couldn't believe what I was hearing!

She finally calmed down. I never heard anything negative after that, thank heavens! If I remember correctly, the only reason we'd been able to get a room so quickly for her was because a resident had died, so one became available in two weeks. Her house sale was closing at the same time, and she had no place else to go. We were lucky to get her situated before our trip out west.

I was 34 years old when we made that trip west. I remember looking in the mirror. My eyes were bloodshot. I was exhausted, worn out emotionally and physically.

The trip out west rejuvenated me. We flew to Calgary, then drove to the coast.

While we were in Victoria, BC, Ron arranged for us to have high tea at the Empress Hotel, where the queen has tea when she visits. It was very thoughtful of him, and it's one of my fondest memories.

Our children were teenagers at the time and didn't want to join us. Funny thing though, after we arrived in BC they didn't want to go back home! They loved the mountains, the Columbia Ice Fields, walking the trails, the Calgary Stampede, Stanley Park and Vancouver. It was, all in all, just a beautiful family vacation, and something we would never forget.

I think Aunt Margaret gave up on life to some extent after moving into that home. She would not get involved in activities and stayed in her room a lot. She'd always been so independent and had lived in the same home for 41 years. I think it was just too much for her to handle.

All I could do was to visit her.

At the time, from 1985-91 I was volunteering as a canvasser for the Cancer Foundation, since my mother had died of leukemia.

In addition, I was volunteering as a play therapist assistant at Centenary Hospital, in the children's ward in 1986-87. I also worked in the geriatric department feeding the elderly and placing fresh water in the patents' rooms. I was working there when I got the call that she had been admitted to a hospital in Toronto.

The hospital called me, as next of kin, to ask me whether they should put feeding tubes into my aunt. In the previous six months she'd suffered several strokes and had been fed by hand tube. She could not talk, feed herself or walk, and she was in the fetal position. It was very sad.

I asked the doctor whether, if they put in the tubes, she would recover. He said no.

Then I made one of the toughest decisions of my life. I instructed them not to put the feeding tubes into Aunt Margaret's body.

They explained that, if they didn't use the tubes, it would not be long before she passed away.

I felt it was the best thing to do under the circumstances. Aunt Marg had been a strong, independent woman all her life, and the last thing she would want was to live like that.

I was certain that letting her go was the right thing to do.

On January 24, 1987 Margaret Armstrong McConkey (Barclay) Marshall died at the age of 90. She was the last of her immediate family to pass away. She had been the youngest of her siblings.

Before she died, when we knew she would not live much longer, we made all of her arrangements. My brother's mother-in-law worked for a funeral parlour and she suggested that we do this in advance, because she'd seen so many times how hard it was for families to take care of the arrangements in the midst of grief. It was a good suggestion, and we were able to take care of everything before the shock of loss took hold.

Margaret had made it clear to me she wished to be cremated. However, for the funeral, you still had to have a display casket. So I ordered a closed casket with a photograph of my Aunt Margaret displayed on top.

My aunt had specifically asked me to scatter her ashes over her family's graves at the Sixth Line Cemetery, where she had already ordered her monument with her name and date of birth on it. I did as she asked, thinking it was an unusual request.

Aunt Margaret was always entrepreneurial in spirit, a woman who was known to think outside of the box. By her 90th birthday, she had suffered six strokes and had spent the final six months in the hospital. I am not sure she even knew who I was. It didn't appear as though she did.

~Chapter Nine~

After Aunt Margaret died, my life changed dramatically. I was a very immature woman of 37 who had no training regarding money or property. I was not ready for the changes about to occur.

In the fall of 1986 I went back to school, to Sheridan College, to take a florist course. I had taken an aptitude test that indicated that would be one of my high aptitudes. I finished the course in 1987 after going to several co-op placements. At The Flower Loft I designed a Halloween display. I decorated the Dean's church for Christmas with the help of one of our teachers, designed arrangements for staff luncheons. The last co-op placement was at Helen Blakely Flowers, and when I finished the course they offered me a full time job.

My self-esteem was still pitifully low. I convinced myself I wasn't good enough, in spite of their having offered me the job.

I thought it would be too hard on me, standing on cement floors all day. Also, I told myself I didn't like the fact you had to work on holidays.

When I got home every day from working in the placements, I was exhausted and in tears. My children wanted me to quit, but I knew that would be teaching them the wrong lesson so I stuck it out. To this day, I don't know why I cried so much. I actually did pretty well at it all. I passed every course except math, and would only have needed that one more credit in order to open my own flower shop.

But I decided not to go back for that one credit.

The reason I could afford this full education was because, when our great aunt died, she left almost her entire estate to my brother Ken and me. Although my father was her nephew, he hadn't been a big part of her life in later years, and she didn't want to leave him anything. But Ken and I had helped her, so she left the bulk to us.

I did convince her to leave at least a token to my father, rather than leaving him out entirely. So she left him a small amount, $5,000.

All of her property, including half of the Orr Lake, were left to Ken and me. The only exception was the property which included her cottage, which she sold prior to her passing. Other than the small sum of $5,000., my father had been overlooked.

This of course drove Teivel into a rage. She blamed me for the way Aunt Margaret had set up her will.

However, I spoke to Margaret's lawyer, and I knew for a fact she had always intended to leave my father out of her will. She did not like the way he and Teivel had shunned Ken and me after our mother died. She was disgusted with the way they used their religion to shut us out of their lives. Also, my father was far too busy with meetings to spend any time with his aunt.

She was a smart woman, and she could see that Teivel lusted after her money. Margaret had no children of her own, and wanted her estate to go to her relatives. She wanted it to be passed down to my children and my brother's children, down her family line.

So Ken and I insured the money, so that no matter what happened, when we died it would be sure to go to our children.

I comforted myself with knowing that at least I'd convinced her not to leave Jack out entirely.

I know you are not supposed to have regrets, but of course I have my share. One of the biggest regrets of my life is that we didn't keep the Orr Lake property.

Also, I didn't speak up when Margaret wanted to sell the cottage. I should have insisted that she sell it to me, but her mind seemed made up and again, my lack of self-esteem got in my way.

Aunt Margaret had it in her head that Ron and I couldn't afford it anyway, and maybe she was right, but because I never thought to ask, we never got the chance.

This trademark lack of communication seems to follow me around and cause trouble for me. Let's face it: it was her property to do with as she wished. I just wish I'd had the guts to bring the subject up. Who knows? With Orr Lake as a family getaway over the years, things might have turned out very differently.

We'll never know!

In the winter of 1987, I also lost another very dear friend. JC died from cancer, which had plagued her for 12 years. She'd been operated on twice already, but could not be operated on again. She decided against chemotherapy.

When I got the sad news, we ended up traveling in one of the worst snowstorms of the year to Sherbrooke, Quebec. Ron made the trip without question, making sure I was able to pay my respects. I've always appreciated him doing that

We managed to cross the bridge just before they closed it for the night.

JC was only 40 years old. I'd met her in our first apartment building, when she was pregnant with her second child, and I with my first.

To this day, I miss her dearly, though I hardly understand it myself.

With that inheritance in my pocket, we decided to take a family vacation to Florida. The children were 17 and 14. However, it was different with teenagers, not as much fun as it had been when they were little. Throughout the years, we had taken them many places, including Florida, the west coast, the east coast, Dominican Republic and Venezuela, so they had a pretty good life.

But we never took them to Florida with us again after that year.

After completing the florist course, I renovated our kitchen. We'd lived in the house since 1972. I added maple cupboards, and two stained glass inserts in the corner cabinets. I replaced the old back door with brick and an octagon window, and instead added a sliding glass door that led out to a new deck.

I made the kitchen larger by removing the laundry room and moving it downstairs to my ceramic room in the basement. There was plenty of room for me to work on my ceramics and still provide enough space for the laundry. In fact, there was even enough space downstairs to use as an extra bedroom, if needed.

Ron found a contractor to do the work in 1988. The contractor did the kitchen renovation in good weather, so Ron would be able to barbeque. I think I may have blocked out the total cost of the work. However, it did turn out beautifully, they did great work. It was wonderful for the family to be able to entertain, and there was a lot more space for a growing family. The old kitchen cabinets were worn out and no longer shut properly, and the kitchen was just too small for us by then.

So my inheritance money came at a good time, when we could really put it to good use.

Although I didn't realize it then, the money was more of a curse than a blessing. Having the money fuelled a sense of power in me, and I was getting too big for my britches. It felt liberating; I felt rich. Ron kept reminding me I was getting too cocky.

I didn't want to think of myself that way, and I truly hated Ron saying that to me. In some ways it was good to have the money, and in other ways it was stifling, there was too much responsibility in making decisions on how to spend the money. Plus some of the people in our circle became envious of us.

As it turned out, I think I made the wrong decision to sell the Orr Lake property. My brother and I both regretted that.

In May of 1988 or 1989, I.B.M. sent Ron down to San Antonio to work for a month. I asked if I could join him for a week, since it was my birthday. I could fly down alone and he could pick me up at the airport, because his room was already paid for, so we only had the cost of the flight to deal with.

We left our teenaged sons home alone, with my brother Ken living just down the street and able to look in on them.

Ron and I had a great time. I shopped in the daytime while he was working, and in the evening we went dancing and he showed me the sights.

Ron even got me a birthday cake. We celebrated around the pool. It was one of the best times of my life.

In 1989 I was working at Zellers in the Bedding and Linen department as a sales consultant. I resigned in December, 1989, after the Christmas rush. I wanted to do something else, but I didn't know what.

I was also a Girl Guide assistant from 1989-1990. My niece was in the Guides and begged me to volunteer, as the unit was desperate for help.

At around this time, our eldest son was beginning a degree course in Graphic Art at Community College in Toronto. Also, our second son started attending Sheridan in a two year course in Photography. Because of the generous inheritance from our Great Aunt to my brother and myself, I was also able to pay for our sons' education.

Thinking back, though, our second son was never really very academically inclined. If I hadn't sprayed him with water every morning, he would not have gotten out of bed and completed high school. Also, he neglected his paperwork to get into college and I had to help him with the forms.

I warned him that he had only one chance to complete his college courses. If he didn't gear up and get through, the money would not keep flowing. I had serious questions about whether he would work hard enough at the courses, and whether he would be able to cope.

At the time, I tried to ignore the danger signs, but it turned out I was right. He partied instead of working hard, and was kicked out of the program after a year.

He had a lot of excuses. It was everyone's fault, but not his. I was at a loss as to what to do with him.

One day he announced that he and his friends were going to join the Army, and through them get a paid education. I was in shock! I really could not see him in the Army, but he was insistent.

Ron and I talked it over, and eventually thought maybe it would be a good idea after all. He might learn some needed discipline, something we'd been unable to teach him, and it might make a man of him.

Our youngest son completed the basic training course, but at one point he came home very upset over what the Army was putting him through, and said that our marital problems were also getting to him.

At that point, I was sure it was too much for him. He said he had talked to his superior office and explained what was going on in his life.

He was told that if he could at least complete the course, he would be given an honourable discharge. He completed, and became a great gunman. They would have been happy to have him go on, but he said it was not for him. We were glad that he stuck with the training, in spite of everything. Of course, at the time, we had no idea of the demons our youngest son was dealing with. I don't think even he understood, as he had blocked out a lot of what had happened to him.

When I think back, it makes sense why our youngest could not get his act together. After Ron and I split up, Ron continually re-enforced his bad behaviour by handing him money to go out to bars and drink away his worries, instead of taking a firm hand and making him get a job and pay for his own expenses.

Ron wanted to be a friend to our boys, instead of a father figure. He had difficulty handing out discipline.

Thank heavens life stepped in, as it often does, and changed our youngest for the better. At the time we felt hopeless, unable to see the forest for the trees.

Our oldest son, by contrast, showed great discipline and worked hard at his three year course, and excelled. He graduated at the top of his class. I don't think he realized how good he was, and like me, he suffered from confidence issues. Also, at his first job, some of the employees teased him about being young and inexperienced.

He couldn't handle the teasing, and was going through a lot emotionally. He wasn't able to easily express himself. In that way, he was very much like Ron. Although he had worked hard and succeeded, he suffered from a learning disability, dyslexia, which he was teased about all through his life. He wasn't formally diagnosed till adulthood, so neither Ron and I or our son really understood what the problem was.

It frustrated him, and he got into fights, especially while in high school. As is often the case with sufferers of dyslexia, our son had above-average intelligence.

An average person might not have been able to handle what had been handed to our son. But he worked hard and eventually found ways to overcome his reading difficulties. He did exceptionally well at math and art, and was very good with his hands, fixing things and carpentry, or electronics. He was also flexible when it came to new jobs, learning new skills easily, like roofing and many other skills.

He did have troubles, and sometimes wasn't sure how to deal with them. But eventually he was hired at a large company. He was a hard worker who looked after his money well. When he married, he provided well for his family and kept the bills paid.

His strong sense of discipline serves him well. He manages his money, is a good cook, can clean the house and look after himself and his family.

His one flaw is that he doesn't always look after himself. He has a tendency to overwork himself, although he is relaxing more with age. He has grown into wonderful man with a terrific family, who feels lucky to have him as a husband and father.

I'd like to point out that many famous people suffer from dyslexia and cope very well: Tom Cruz, Whoopi Goldberg, Cher and many more.

I'm so glad this disorder is now being recognized and treated, and that the stigma is slowly being removed.

In the fall of 1990, I decided to return to college and take courses in Home Furnishings and Fashion Merchandising. I'd always wanted to work in interior decoration. The children were 22 and 20, and no longer needed me in the same way. Also, I still had the money from my inheritance and could afford the course. I also decided to finally obtain my driver's licence, just before starting the courses.

I had asked Ron to teach me to drive, but after one session, it was clear that wouldn't work. He didn't have the patience and it really hurt my confidence.

I needed a teacher who would build my confidence up, not tear it down. He didn't mean to do it, but that was the effect, so I said no thanks to any further sessions.

Even after I'd gotten my licence, I was still too nervous to drive to school, so I took the bus and subway while attending my courses.

I wasn't able to pass my driving test the first time, and that also really hurt my confidence. I felt like a failure, and asked my instructor what I should do next? He said, "I'm going to book you another appointment and we're going to continue practicing and then you are going to pass the test and get your licence."

That's exactly what I did, two weeks later!

I couldn't believe it! It was a sunny January day, January 12, 1991. The evening after I got my licence we had been invited to the birthday party of a friend of Ron's, and I was appointed as the designated driver. So everyone at the party was drinking except for me, which was really weird, being sober among a group who had been drinking.

It was my first experience being sober among a group who wasn't. It was really weird and everyone around me looked like they were nuts!

It made me realize the huge responsibility I had as a driver. Thank goodness I never needed a drink to have a good time at a party.

Once I started driving regularly, there was no stopping me. Just to have the freedom of having wheels, and being able to pick up and go whenever you like, is a very powerful thing.

I was working very hard at my two year course in Home Furnishings and Fashion Merchandising. I really wanted to succeed at that. I did very well in the courses and exams and was chosen as Mentor for the Home Furnishings program, because I was such a dedicated and responsible student.

When I look back on it now, I see what a huge compliment that was. I was considered someone who my classmates could turn to for help and advice and to set an example.

I designed a recycling store using a retail store concept. Our instructor cautioned us to choose a store concept we felt strongly about, as we'd be working with it for two years. The first year we would design the store, and the second year we would plan inventory levels.

We worked from a standard student manual for IBM PC by Ruth Keyes. The workbook provided case study locations, demographics and cost factors.

I knew that the environment and recycling was becoming very important in the public mind, and I definitely felt strongly about saving the environment. So I decided to create a Recycling Store. My design carried many categories of products that all were related to protecting the environment. We had products to do with composting and other natural items.

My design featured a quiet atmosphere, enhanced by the addition of a tropical rainforest creation and a waterfall coming down the wall in the centre of the store, to draw customer attention. Audio tapes would provide the appropriate sounds and atmospheric scents would complete the effect.

I used skylights to provide natural light and encourage the forest growth. The floor was made of recycled tires, wallpaper was environmentally friendly and contained no mercury.

The primary décor features would be living foliage, such as herbs, plants, flowers and trees. The main colour theme would be white and green.

One percent of all earned revenue would be contributed to environmental causes

We worked as a group on the Recycling Caddy, but the idea was mine. It was to be sold in my store. It was to be used in kitchens.

I was nominated for the Fashion Bursary Award where I presented my idea to a panel of judges.

This was before "recycling" was a fully accepted notion in society. The notion of environmental protection was in its infant stages.

Our school ended up competing with other schools. The competition narrowed to seven schools, and I went downtown to present my plan and products to a panel of several people. I was very nervous. But I did my best and came in either second or third.

In second year, I chose to work at Eaton's Model Home with a designated designer. She also had a junior designer and we three worked well together. After completing my co-op time, I did a presentation about the Gibbard Furniture Company that Eaton's often featured in their show. Gibbard's specialized in traditional furniture.

I was given the opportunity to interview the owner of the store, and took some photos of him with his designs. I was later allowed to use these photos and information for my presentation back at school.

The designer I worked with said she thought I would be a very good designer. She advised me to first get a job selling furniture, to increase my knowledge. She said she would put in a good word for me with human resources.

Unfortunately, she died soon afterward, and wasn't able to help me out that way. Her Lupus came back with a vengeance, at the young age of 37.

While she was in the hospital, I sent flowers to cheer her. I attended her funeral, which was very sad. She left behind a husband and two very young daughters.

There are no appropriate words for those occasions. Nothing I could say would ever bring her back.

In April of 1991 our class traveled to New York City to see the Fashion District. We went into Brunschwig & Fils, a place that designs patterns for wallpaper, as well as offers forecasts for upcoming fashion and colour trends.

We saw the estate of the Vanderbilt's, a glass factory and a lot of designer furniture. It was quite an experience! I also went to a Neil Simon play and to the famous Hard Rock Café, where the bartender bought me a drink.

I remember feeling weird about that, and almost refused the drink, but my classmates said there was no harm in it, accept it and say thanks! I did feel flattered to be hit on, which might seem silly, but I wasn't used to this happening to me, so it was a surprise.

Our teacher had arranged for us to visit a jazz club, or speak easy, as it would have been called in the '20s. We traveled in taxies, four to a cab, and felt a definite buzz of excitement around being in New York City. You could feel the excitement everywhere, especially in Times Square and the entertainment district! I also went to Greenwich Village to see what all the fuss was about. I used the restroom in Trump Tower to check it out. There was Carrara marble, in a rust shade mixed with white, from the floor to the counters, and the gold sinks were very opulent. It all seemed to be a big deal at the time.

These days, given the news, I would probably pass right by and not be quite as impressed.

However, I was there to learn about decorating and architecture, and in that field Trump was a genius. Too bad he didn't stick to that.

Gail's Great Aunt Margaret (Barclay) Marshall

Gail's paternal grandparents, Zeta (Barclay) & Telford Sharpe
Wedding Day, August 30, 1916

Baby Evelyn Arloah Sharpe with mother Zeta Sharpe, 1917

John Sharpe/Ellen Gray Family, 1878 Simcoe Archives
Gail's great-great paternal grandparents in centre,
Great paternal grandfather, Matthew Gray Sharpe,
Back row, far right, standing

Gail's mother's parents and siblings

Irene (Petch) and Jack Sharpe, 1941

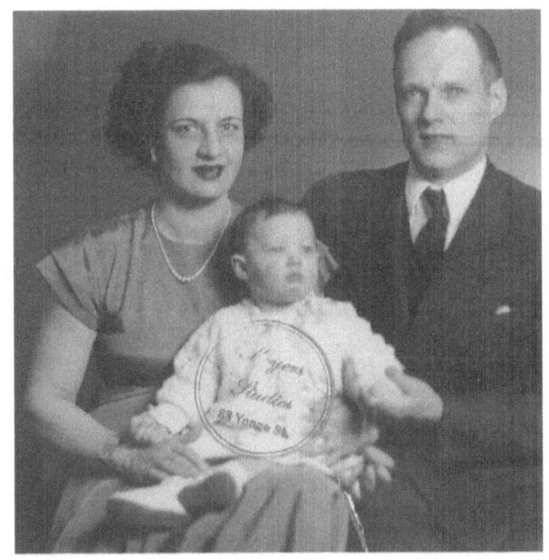

Irene & Jack Sharpe with baby Gail Louise

Christmas family gathering, 1951

Gail Sharpe with baby brother Kenneth

Gail on stairs, Great Aunt Kit above
Photo carried all the time by Great-Aunt Marg

Kenneth & Gail Sharpe, 7 Marsh Rd.

Gail riding a bike

Gail with a cat

Gail at Orr Lake, 1953

Gail at Orr Lake cottage

Gail's award-winning garden, 1959

Jack Sharpe with Ken and Gail, Orr Lake

Orr Lake cottage, 1950s

Gail at Orr Lake, 1966 or '67

Gail Sharpe and Ron Kelly, 1967

Irene, Gail and Jack Sharpe

Jack Sharpe and daughter Gail

Bridesmaids, Matron of Honour, Gail and father Jack Sharpe

Jack and Gail Sharpe

Gail's mother and brother

Gail and Ron with Gail's parents

Gail and Ron with Ron's mother

Ron and Gail Kelly with wedding party, Kingdom Hall

Ronald William Kelly and Gail Louise Sharpe, Wedding Day

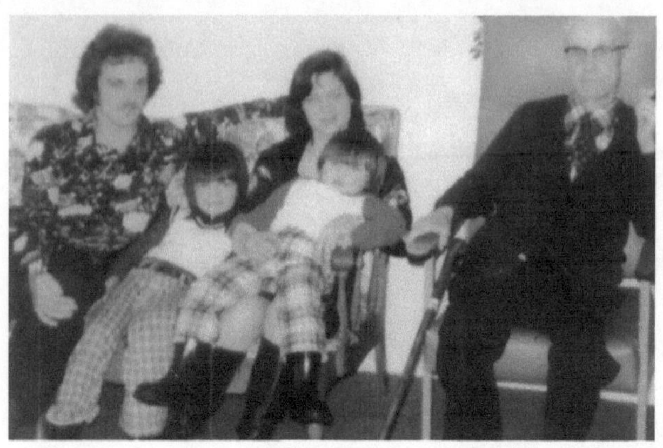

Ken Sharpe and sister Gail Kelly with her sons, first meeting Gail's grandfather Telford Sharpe

Jack Sharpe at Jehovah's Witness Convention

Gail Louise Sharpe Kelly, 1984

Kenneth John Sharpe and sister Gail Sharpe Kelly, 1995

Gail on her 2nd wedding day

~Chapter Ten~

By the time I finished my education, my marriage was on its last legs. Ron and I were drifting further and further apart. We had nothing in common anymore, and couldn't even seem to talk to each other. Every night when he got home from work, Ron headed straight to the rec room in the basement to watch TV.

I'd been too busy with my schoolwork and shopping to pay attention, and ended up going in an entirely different direction.

So when a young man, a friend of my son's, paid attention to me, I let it go to my head. All he was doing was being polite. His mother had instilled in him a love of antiques, and we shared that common interest. He wanted to learn about the treasures we had in our home that had been handed down to us.

Our friendship was right out in the open, and Ron didn't seem to care.

At one point my interest in the young man must have become obvious, because my son started dropping hints that I should leave him and his friend alone. I paid no attention, until suddenly I realized I was going overboard and called a friend for advice.

She suggested that I could speak to a psychologist. I realized that I had a problem, harbouring such feelings for a man my son's age, and I wanted to understand and get help.

I felt terrible about the whole situation and called my son's friend to explain as best I could. I told him I liked him a lot, but I knew my feelings were inappropriate and nothing would come of it. I asked him to be discreet.

After the previous incident, I really didn't want Ron to know.

I continued to see the psychologist the whole time I was taking my courses.

I'm not sure when we made the decision to visit Myrtle Beach. I had purchased a white Dodge convertible in 1991, with a burgundy interior. We took my car and drove south; Ron did the driving.

We'd never been to Myrtle Beach before. I think it was Ron's idea to go there, but I'm not sure. My guess is that he was trying to put the spark back in our marriage.

Earlier, Ron had arranged for us to visit a divorce lawyer. I'd broken down in the lawyer's office, and it was clear I wasn't quite ready for divorce. The lawyer suggested we take the trip we had arranged together and see whether we could work things out.

Myrtle Beach was beautiful, and the weather was great, but it was obvious Ron had already made up his mind. He was distant and angry and would not sleep with me. He accused me of sleeping with my psychologist, which was nonsense. I told him if that was the case my treatment should be free!

He couldn't understand why I'd been seeing the psychologist so often, so I broke down and told him about my inappropriate feelings for our son's friend. I explained that I knew full well it was wrong and that's why I was seeking help.

All in all, Ron was finished with me. He didn't want to sleep with me and we hadn't been happy in a long while. The young man became an excuse, and he said the marriage was over.

I was dumb-founded. So much for working on our marriage. The trip was a waste of money.

I remembered that my psychologist had warned me specifically not to confide my feelings about the young man to Ron. He warned Ron would definitely not understand. Looking back, I suspect Ron felt worthless and left out of our marriage at that point. I had always confided in him in the past, probably more than I should, but about this I'd not said a word.

One of the first things my doctor asked about was my childhood. In talking with him, it was like a part of my brain opened up. It really hurt. I have never before or since experienced anything like that. I believe I had blocked out a lot of childhood memories, and now this doctor was encouraging me to open those doors.

This doctor helped me far more than I knew at the time. As you read on, you'll come to understand why I say this.

At the time, he suggested I should try to reconcile with Ron. I was flabbergasted! I said no way was I going to put myself through all that again, when things would likely not change or improve. I didn't see how Ron and I could ever resolve our differences.

I guess my psychologist saw something I didn't see.

One of the hardest things was to tell our grown sons that we could not work it out and that we were separating. There is no manual to tell you what to say, how to handle this situation. It was terribly sad and painful for our children as well as for both of us.

I saw some condos for sale near our family home. There was a huge sale and the price had been dropped around $100,000. I visited a few times to look them over and get a sense of the various floor plans and cost. Even though I was feeling very low about the end of our marriage, I felt drawn to one layout in particular. I asked

Ron to come and look at it with me, for a second opinion.

It might seem strange, my asking my ex-husband for advice in this way, but he came. He was still the decent, good man I had married. We'd just been through too much together, that's all.

Ron thought it was both a nice place and a good deal. He said that in his opinion, it was the kind of place I would be happy to stay in the rest of my life. It didn't hurt that it was still in the neighbourhood of our grown children and our former family home.

I said I didn't have enough money left for the down payment. Ron offered to lend me $5,000. And when the divorce was final, we could deduct that amount from the settlement.

That seemed sensible, so I agreed. I bought the condo.

It had one bedroom, one bathroom with a separate shower and bathtub, a den, living room, dining room and galley kitchen. The kitchen passed into the dining room, and the laundry room had a stackable washer and dryer.

No one had ever lived in this condo. It was brand new. It overlooked a green space park and a train track that was hardly ever used. Even though the building was a high rise, my condo was on the second floor, so it had the feeling of looking out the upstairs window of a house. I could easily take the stairs, which was good, and we were in walking distance from my doctor's office and grocery, pharmacy and a small plaza.

Most importantly, it was very close to where our sons were living. Even though they were grown, in fact our eldest was dating, they still lived in the family home and I would never consider taking them out of their home.

Also, I thought they would be better off with their father at this point, as they were very close to leaving the nest.

I remember all the packing I had to do. As I packed, Ron, my brother Ken and his wife all sat in the front of the house drinking, laughing and having a great old time. I felt like I didn't exist, like no one loved me or cared what I was doing.

That feeling kept running through my mind. Also I was angry that Ron got to stay in the home I had created. The fact that he and my own brother seemed to be having a great time and not thinking of me at all was just icing on a very sour cake.

On September 24, 1992, I moved to the condo. Our kids and their friends helped me move, and Ron insisted on controlling the situation by giving instructions. He said he would stay at the house and organize everyone. I tried to tell him he didn't need to do that, but he insisted and I finally gave up and let him do his thing.

When the move was finished, I went back to the house to order pizza for everyone who had helped. I went downstairs where Ron was and was about to knock on the bathroom door to tell him the pizza was on its way, when suddenly I heard him crying inside.

I felt terrible. I wanted to console him, to tell him we could call the whole thing off, it wasn't too late!

But I couldn't bring myself to do it. What if he laughed at me? What if he rejected me again like he had at Myrtle Beach? I'd feel like a fool all over again, and I couldn't put myself in that position. I could not be the one to call Uncle.

So I pretended not to hear him crying, and knocked on the door and said "Pizzas are here."

Isn't there a saying about "Pride cometh before a fall?"

It was a completely screwed up time. To give you an idea, the day after I'd moved out I was broke, had no money whatsoever. I had spent my last dollar buying pizza the day before. I was crying uncontrollably.

I called Ron to ask if he could lend me some money for groceries, and drive me to the store. I explained I couldn't stop crying long enough to drive myself.

He agreed, and took me to the store. I cried the entire time I was shopping.

I called my psychologist and told him that I couldn't stop crying. He advised me to make an appointment immediately at the hospital to get a prescription, as I couldn't go around crying like that all the time. I have no idea which medication was prescribed. I only know I was desperate, and I took it.

Leaving my home after 20 years, the home where I'd raised my children, was the hardest time of my life. It really tore my heart out to leave my sons and our home. I felt I had no other choice. Ron would not talk to me, and he wouldn't talk with a marriage counsellor.

If someone will not talk, there is no hope to work things out. At least I didn't know of another way. It seemed like a no-win situation to me. Ron was in pain. I was in pain. The only alternative I saw was to leave and divorce. I hoped the pain would eventually go away.

I felt isolated. My family didn't approve of my decision. I felt there was nowhere to turn and no one I could talk to. Although I never openly admitted it, I used anger to fuel my desire to leave. I was convinced I was in the right, and did not take any responsibility for where we ended up. Feeling I was right is what got me out the door and into a new life.

No matter how lonely I was, and no matter that I had no one to confide in, I felt empty but I put on a happy face and pretended everything was going to be okay.

I blamed Ron completely for our divorce. He wouldn't talk. That is what caused it.

To this day, I still ask myself whether I should have done things differently. Did I have any control over the way things had turned out? Did I make the right decision that day, in not comforting Ron?

There are not many U-turns allowed in life. Once some major decisions are made and implemented, you usually cannot turn back the clock and re-do things. Your life is changed forever. You find yourself on a different path.

I carried a lot of resentment over the fact that Ron got to still live with our sons, even though I always knew it was the most sensible thing. I resented losing Ron, my rock, my father-figure, the man who was always there for me in a way my father had never been.

Ron had always been my protector, and in the earlier days he had been my lover. I resented the fact that I'd given up those things forever.

My justification was that I was right. He would not talk and because of that nothing could be resolved.

My "rightness" was a fatal flaw. When we are caught up in being right, nothing can move ahead, nothing can be resolved. I didn't know that then, or maybe I didn't want to see the truth.

The notion of being right seemed more important to me at the time than anything else.

I remember I finally started to think about this clearly after seeing a Dr. Phil show. In the show, Dr. Phil talked about marriage and infidelity. He argued that, if one partner was unfaithful, it was often better to stay together, try to truly forgive and work things out, even if you later find you can't stay forever.

He argued that, if you just give up and leave the marriage, you take your own problems with you all unresolved, and will likely repeat all the same mistakes.

So in Dr. Phil's opinion, it was almost always better in these cases to seek counselling and at least try to work things out, even if it proves impossible. This way you have a fighting chance to learn what your own mistakes and responsibility for the problems were, and have a better chance of doing things right in the future.

I wish I'd seen this episode when Ron was still alive, even if we'd already broken up. I think it would have made a difference in how I looked at things, and in how I treated him.

"What if?" is one of those questions that can really drive you crazy. At some point you have to accept your own errors and flaws and let it go.

But if I was asked for advice by a couple in our situation, I would definitely advise them to try your best to make the marriage work. Don't give up too easily, and don't waste a lot of energy in convincing yourself you are always right.

I've always believed that marriage is supposed to be for life, a contract we make forever. When we broke up, I felt as though I was going against my own belief system, because I was frustrated and didn't know what else to do. I wouldn't listen to my psychologist, wouldn't listen to anyone. I was right and that was that.

I hope that, in some way in heaven, Ron knows that I still love him. I never stopped having that feeling for him, and I probably never will. It will not bring him back, but at least I can now be honest about my feelings and live in tune with them, rather than living in denial.

Ron made the same mistakes that I made. He also didn't try, he didn't encourage me to stay and visit the counsellor.

So we were both wrong. I think he probably regretted it as much as I did.

It was too bad we couldn't see these things clearly at the time.

~Chapter Eleven~

After moving into my new condo, I felt lost and alone and did not fit in. I spent my time painting and decorating my place, but nothing I did made me really happy.

In the fall of 1992 I applied for a job working over Christmas at a kiosk called St. Nick's Place, in the Scarborough Town Centre. We were all to wear Santa's hats. We were taught how to engrave brass ornaments and pewter beer steins, as well as how to etch glass for mugs and glasses. I glued names on children's Christmas stockings, which parents had bought for them.

I was the manager of the store and handled and counted the money, turning it in each night from the till.

I really enjoyed the job! When the two and a half months were finished, they offered me a job in Newmarket, at another St. Nick's Place, but I turned the offer down, thinking it would be too far to drive. To this day I kick myself for turning that down. Live and learn!

Before moving into the condo, I went on a spending spree. As a result, I owed a lot of money on my credit cards. At the time, I wasn't planning ahead, just reacting to the pain and trying to make myself feel better. Of course, the shopping did not make me feel better. All it made me feel was scared at how I was going to pay off the cards. The small amount of excitement the purchases gave me didn't last. I soon felt guilty and afraid.

A friend offered to pay the cards off for me as long as I signed an agreement to pay off the loan in one year with 8% interest in cash. At that time, it was far less interest than I had been paying on the cards, so it was a good deal.

I agreed, but if she had not suggested it, I never would have asked.

Part of the agreement was that I never run up my credit cards again, and I never have.

I was very grateful for the loan, which had come out of nowhere. I was both grateful and relieved.

Seven months later, I asked the same friend if she knew any single men I might be interested in. She had been single for a long time before marrying, so I thought she might know a lot of single people. She said she did know someone, but wasn't sure if he was still single.

So she contacted the man, and it turned out he was still single. He called me and I was very nervous at first, but soon calmed down. He was easy to talk to and we ended up talking for three hours.

We made a date for April 3, 1993 and he was to pick me up and take me to breakfast. I was so nervous I could hardly eat. Then he drove me to Elmira and Elora where the Mennonite communities are, because I'd told him how I loved antiques.

We spent the day walking around, looking at the market and the stores. It was a lovely day. It was exciting, and he had a beautiful smile. He had never been married and had no children.

I didn't like the fact that he was bald, but I decided not to let that put me off. I didn't want to be so judgemental.

After just leaving a 25 year relationship, I should have been putting on the brakes, but of course I didn't do that.

The man seemed happy and easy-going, and there was definitely chemistry between us, but I did have some doubts. There was something about him, but I couldn't put my finger on it. I didn't have the experience.

I was so lonely and starved for affection that I am sure I didn't think too much about it.

Thus began my relationship with the second man in my life.

When I told my psychologist about the new relationship, he said it was far too soon, and I wasn't ready for this new relationship. I told the new boyfriend what my psychologist said, and he of course said the doctor didn't know what he was talking about, that I was ready and not to listen to the doctor. He reassured me that if I wanted to wait, he'd wait for me, but I was so anxious to have a relationship, I didn't want to wait.

As it turned out, the psychologist was right. But I only discovered that later. So I immediately stopped seeing the psychologist and began seeing the new man in earnest.

My new boyfriend moved in with me seven months after we met. He owned nothing of value, no house or property, just an old car. He worked as a postal carrier for Canada Post, just like my father had. He was 37 and in good shape, probably from all the walking he did for his job. He was seven years younger than me. I never questioned the fact that he had nothing, I guess he just spent it as quickly as he earned it.

He wanted to move in with me in November of 1993, but I had already booked a flight to Florida. I was to stay for a week in Florida with a girlfriend. He thought it would be fine to just move in while I was out of town, but I said absolutely not! He would have to wait till I got back.

That should have been another clue for me about him.

I had a co-habitation agreement made up and I needed him to sign it before he moved in. He argued that it wasn't necessary, that he wouldn't give me any trouble. I insisted it was like spilt milk: It's too late after the milk is on the floor. I made sure he signed it before he moved in, and he finally agreed.

His arguing should have been another red flag, but I kept ignoring the clues! Isn't it interesting how we can do these things to ourselves, all in the name of love? Or maybe I should say "lust".

He finally did sign the document. It's the one thing I did right, making sure he signed the co-habitation agreement before he moved in and before our marriage.

Love is definitely blind!

My eldest son became engaged in the spring of 1993. Even though they'd been dating for a while, I was still surprised to hear of the engagement. Maybe we always think of our children as children, and it comes as a surprise to us when they are all grown up. It happens far too soon, as every parent knows.

The wedding was scheduled for March 1994. It was a large wedding, as the bride's family was Sicilian. I'd originally thought I'd have to attend the wedding alone, but now I had a boyfriend who could attend with me.

When Ron heard I was bringing my new boyfriend, he literally ran out to a bar and found a woman who agreed to attend the wedding with him. He didn't want to be alone when I wasn't.

Ron also had this woman and her daughter move into our family home two weeks before the wedding. Our son and his bride were not happy about this. But it was Ron's decision, we were not together anymore.

Just before the wedding, Ron had an accident at work and nearly cut his finger off. In the receiving line on our son's wedding day, he told each person in the reception about cutting his finger. I was so angry with him, I could have wrung his neck!

I remained calm and quiet, except for speaking with the guests. Before it was over, I had a terrible headache from the strain. Go figure!

My ex-husband had of course been drinking heavily and was at the front of the room with his buddies, singing at a microphone. I felt really uncomfortable, since there were so many friends and family of Ron's there and it brought home the reality of the situation.

Finally, all the hoopla was over. The wedding, the showers, the guests. It was a beautiful ceremony and reception, and another milestone in the raising of our children. So much planning, excitement, organization and work, all for one day, and then it's over, just like that!

I got a job at Avenue Brides as a sales assistant. I'd been working since October, 1993. The store went out of business, and closed in February of 1994, just before our son's wedding. The store was in the Chinese section of Toronto. I wasn't comfortable with the crowds and noise, especially on the bus. The streets were dirty and the smells were unusual. The crowds and noise would reach a screeching pitch, not relaxing at the end of a hard working day.

So when they closed, I admit I was elated that I wouldn't have to go back.

I still had my other job, at Patricia Bridal Salon. I preferred it, because I was not alone when I was working and although the work was hard, it was enjoyable.

~Chapter Twelve~

Ron and I were officially divorced in April, 1994, about a month after our eldest son's wedding. I only now realized the timing!

I believe it was June of 1994 when I became engaged to the new man in my life. We had looked at rings together and I'd chosen what was called an Anniversary Ring, with a wide white gold band and two rows of seven diamonds.

So the ring would be a surprise when the time came for him to propose, he hid it in his pocket. We went to the park and paused at a gazebo. He did his best to make the engagement special, getting down on his knees to pop the question.

And so I was engaged for the second time in my life!

Meanwhile, I continued working at my part-time job at Patricia Bridal Salon, for my friend Dianne who was the owner. I really enjoyed working as a sales assistant and consultant, helping the brides to choose their dresses. The place in Markham was bright and clean, and well decorated, and more important, you could ask for help from the owner if you needed it.

It could be pretty hectic at times, but Dianne was very competent and able to handle any kind of situation. I always felt secure when she was in the store.

Some years later Dianne sold the store, and it's no longer there.

I also started working that May as a consultant for Mary Kay. I did facials, skin care, makeup applications and meetings. I didn't care for the meetings. I lasted in that job for about a year before resigning.

Sometime in 1994, I had answered an ad for a cleaning lady for a home in Markham. I was also cleaning for a lady who was a Realtor, and she told me to let her know if I ever wanted to buy or sell my property.

I would later regret listening to her advice to sell my condo, but at the time I know she meant well. I guess it wasn't all bad.

On October 6, 1994 I was offered another job teaching children from ages eight to fourteen how to make ceramics, clean, paint and glaze. I fired their ceramic pieces in a kiln to complete the job. The classes were offered through the City of Scarborough at Port Union Community Centre, but there weren't enough students to fill the winter semester, so the class ended on December 29, 1994.

I was offered another job teaching adults, but I was too shy and turned it down. If it came up now, I'd have no problem with it. I had the ability and the skills to teach, but I needed to force myself to get over the shyness.

In March 1995, I was hired at B.B. Bargoon's as a part-time sales assistant. The job lasted for just over two weeks. It entailed measuring material, cutting it from large rolls, pricing remnants, and using the computerized cash register. They let me go, and I never understood why. I was devastated. It makes you feel like such a failure, losing a job that way!

While I was dating my second husband, his sister asked me if I'd like to go to a party where there was going to be a psychic. I'd never been to a psychic before, and I agreed to go.

My boyfriend's sister didn't have her fortune read, but I did. The psychic, a man, had long grey hair. I was told he had helped police in the Bernardo case, so I thought he might be legit. I saw him several times after that.

The Jehovah's Witnesses don't believe in going to psychics or fortune tellers or anything like that. Although I don't agree with most JW beliefs, I do agree with them that you should stay away from any black magic. Respect it for what it is and stay away from it.

I do believe in paranormal within reason. I believe in ghosts and spirits, but that doesn't mean I want to contact them. I also believe in evil unexplained phenomena. Like everything in life, there are good and bad things. There are some psychics born with a natural ability who try to do good, and others you should stay away from. You have to be on your guard to know good from bad.

This psychic actually told me, almost to the exact day, when Ron would die. I didn't ask him and didn't want to believe it. I had just showed him pictures of Ron, and he came out with it as soon as he saw the photos, that Ron would die of a heart attack in five years. There was nothing to be done about it, he said. When the heart stops, it stops.

I remember a tear coming down my cheek when he said this. And even though I'd had five years' warning, I was still in shock when Ron died.

I saw this psychic a couple of times, and then he told me I couldn't afford him. I appreciated that, because he was right. He was just being honest about the situation.

I think the main reason I wanted to see a psychic in the first place is because I'd never been allowed in my parents' religion. Or maybe it was just the mystery of it all.

On the morning of my second wedding, I invited my new mother-in-law to come to have her makeup done at my condo. We had champagne and orange juice and quiches for breakfast. I wanted to make it as nice as possible for both her and me on that special day.

My fiancé went out early before the cameraman arrived and his mother arrived before the makeup artist and hairdresser. That way we could spend the time alone, without my fiancé. We would have time to relax before the limousine arrived to take me, my matron of honour and my mother-in-law to the church for the service.

We had been engaged for about a year when we were married at Saint Andrews Presbyterian Church, the oldest church in Scarborough. I chose it because of its quaint setting on a quiet street, in a green space. It was the end of July, 1995. Another beautiful day.

Our reception was at the picturesque Guild Inn, looking over Lake Ontario. It was surrounded with sculptures, a wishing well and beautiful gardens.

I ordered a wooden floor to be placed outdoors for dancing, and it was covered by a large tent.

Everything was perfect, it seemed.

I wore an ivory silk skirt and an off-the-shoulder top made by my friend Dianne. She also made a small matching purse in the same fabric, and little silk roses to go into the back of my hair. It came with a jacket that went with the skirt. I wore that in the church and then changed into the off-the-shoulder top for the reception.

As before, I bought my dress on sale, this time at the Patricia Bridal Salon which was owned by Dianne. Dianne was also my matron of honour; I'd known her since our children were babies. She wore a long pink dress.

My fiancé and his best man wore black tuxedos, as did my sons, who were groomsmen, and my brother, who walked me down the aisle. I did send an invitation to my father, but got no response. My guess is that Teivel destroyed it.

At that point, I really didn't care whether my father came or not. He wasn't part of my life, and I sure didn't want his wife to come.

We had hired a limousine for the day, and it took us back to the condo, so we could pick up our bags. Then it took us to the airport for our flight to Jamaica the next morning.

It's all a blur now. I was very tired, and let's just say the wedding night was nothing to write home about, a real disappointment after all the hoopla.

Then I got a bright idea! I decided to sell my condo, which was really too small for the two of us, especially with all my husband's things now in it. Besides, I was used to living in a house. I believe I must have been thinking of it ever since he moved in, because I really didn't like the congested feeling of all of his things being in my small place.

I don't think I mentioned it to him until that moment. I'd been cleaning for a lady who was a realtor, and she'd offered to help if I ever wanted to sell. This was about 1996.

I told her I wanted a house that looked just like the one on *Father Knows Best*. She said she knew exactly what I meant and delivered up a cute three bedroom house in Uxbridge. It was a quaint, up-and-coming area that I really loved.

I put all of the money from the sale of my condo down on the new house. My husband had nothing, and refused even to help with the mortgage payments, saying he didn't have enough money. So, like a fool, I paid half the mortgage payments even though I'd made the entire down payment.

This was my third big mistake, and it was a whopper! If I was faced with this decision again, I would have demanded an immediate annulment or divorce. In the long run, it would have been cheaper. I would have suffered the embarrassment of such a short marriage, but I would have gotten over it, with a lot less frustration.

Should have. Could have. Would have. If only.

We moved into the house in March of 1996 and lived there for three and half years, about the same length of time I'd lived in my condo.

I woke up crying, and was depressed, and didn't know why. I never told anyone. But I think deep down I knew I shouldn't be there, with him.

I was scared. I knew I had to make a change, but then I would have to admit I'd made a mistake by having my boyfriend move in in the first place. I'd also have to kick my husband out on his ear.

My brain was in denial and wouldn't allow me to contemplate any of this. I was walking around in a dream or illusion of what I thought this relationship was.

I couldn't deal with living in an illusion of a marriage, but I also couldn't contemplate that it had been a huge mistake! I don't deal with making mistakes very well, and I wouldn't let myself believe this had been a doozy!

So I just kept up the façade, pretending that everything was rolling along wonderfully and there were no problems.

Without realizing what I was doing or why, I just went on with my life, pretending I had no cares in the world. That everything was all right within my world.

In the summer of 1996 a member of my family and his wife decided to buy a cottage on a lake. When you purchase a cottage, you must put down 35%. As they could not come up with the whole amount, they asked me if they could borrow some money for a year.

I was happy to help. I spoke with my financial manager, who suggested that I ask for an interest rate on top of what they borrowed, so I did. I also told them if it was too hard to pay it back in a year, they could take longer. But they insisted a year would be okay, and they borrowed the money.

I was happy to do it, but I learned later they didn't like the fact I'd asked for interest. I explained to them that my money wouldn't be invested for a year and I'd be losing that interest.

Thinking back, I realized that if my Great Aunt Margaret had not left Ken and me a generous inheritance, I would not have been able to help this family member or anyone else. We owed her a lot of gratitude for that. I'll never forget her and I sure do appreciate what she did for me.

I just wish I could have spoken with her about finances, and learned more about how to handle them before receiving the inheritance.

Then my new husband also asked me to loan him money for a year. This made me wonder whether he'd married me for my money. I didn't have a lot, but he seemed to think I did.

After I'd been in Uxbridge for about a year, I met a lady who sold me blinds in my home. I began spending time with her and we became friends. She showed me around our town.

I started working for Community Care cleaning for the elderly, a job that allowed me the flexibility of changing locations when I moved. In all, I worked for them for 16 years.

I also did a lot of Reflexology, cleansing, meditation, and took a dowsing course. I generally did my best to take care of myself.

I decorated, painted and wallpapered the house and took pride in looking after my new home, just as I had all my others. I even designed and hand-painted a banner for the main street to advertise art in Uxbridge. The town supplied the banner and I had the paint needed to complete the job. I really enjoyed it!

Meanwhile, my husband cared for the outside work, trimming the lawn, watering and working on projects in our garage. I give my husband credit for his hard work and for always holding down a job as well. For a while, it appeared as though our marriage would last.

I was so wrong.

In January of 1997 I convinced my husband to attend a Computer Literacy class with me at Durham College. I wanted to learn more about computers at the time, as I was bored, and wanted to buy a PC and learn to use it properly. Although he was reluctant, he took the course with me.

~Chapter Thirteen~

In the fall of 1997 I received the fantastic news that I was going to be a grandmother! My first grandchild was due in May, 1998. Needless to say I was ecstatic, because my son and his wife had talked about the possibility of not having children. I had almost given up on grandchildren, and this was a welcome surprise.

My eldest son and daughter-in-law asked me to be in the delivery room with them. They felt that her mother was too excitable and would not be a calming influence. I wasn't sure I could handle it, but told them I'd think about it.

Then I got the call: the baby was on the way! I drove down early in the morning to the hospital in Ajax. On the way, I decided I didn't want to miss the chance to be present for the birth. I felt I could handle whatever might happen.

My daughter-in-law had been given the anesthetic too early, and could not be given any more. I left the room to fetch ice for her to suck on to help, and lo and behold, there was my ex-husband trying to help me, get the ice. It was very surreal.

We were, after all this time, still working together in an unusual circumstance.

My daughter-in-law felt exhausted, and said she could not continue. I told her not to give up, she was really close. I encouraged her to push, which she did, and suddenly there he was, my grandson!

His body was red, his hair black. He had huge hands and feet and looked so strong. His cries were loud and strong, too. I believe he was bigger and looked stronger than either of my sons had at birth.

I felt an immediate connection to this new member of our family, a bond that would transcend my life. What a fantastic miracle! What a gift this was to the rest of us! I was so glad I'd decided to be present for the birth, a memory I'll hold onto forever.

My son cut his son's umbilical cord and I was so proud of him. It was something I'd wanted Ron to do when our sons were born, but for his own reasons he chose not to, and I know he later regretted that decision.

My daughter-in-law had lost a lot of blood. She appeared very pale, and was exhausted. She'd opted not to watch the birth, and everyone is different in these matters. I loved watching my sons being born, and my grandson as well!

I was so grateful to them for including me in the day. I was grateful to be alive, and to be enjoying this tremendous privilege.

I went to the waiting room, to break the news to the rest of the family: everyone was OK, and the family had a brand new baby boy! My younger son congratulated me for being in the room to support his brother and sister-in-law.

By that point, I was whipped. My husband had arrived at the hospital, and we went out for a late dinner. I remember thinking at the time that this was a truly fantastic and memorable day, and one that would likely never be repeated.

So far, nothing like this has ever happened since. I'll always treasure that experience!

I must have mentioned at some time to my husband that I would like to live near a lake. He put in for a transfer to Peterborough, and to my surprise he got it. All of a sudden, I had to put our home up for sale and prepare to move again!

I really wasn't prepared to do that so soon. I asked for advice from my family, and thought long and hard. In the end I did make the move.

This is a lesson we all need to learn: to listen to ourselves when we are feeling reluctant, to give credit to our gut instincts.

I say this now, after everything I've gone through.

So we set out to find a place near his work, preferably on a lake. The realtor who had found our house in Uxbridge came to help us sell it, and also put us in touch with a realtor in the Kawarthas to search for a new house.

The day we headed out to look at houses, I had my period and felt lousy. I wasn't really interested in looking that day. However, my husband was gung ho and especially liked one of the places we looked at.

It was only OK in my opinion. It had both good things and bad things about it, but to my eyes, it was very dated, needed a lot of work, and didn't have a furnace.

He loved it the way it was. Of course, he had no sense of style, and no idea of what was dated or up to date.

I said I couldn't live in it the way it was. If we bought it, we would have to renovate. He agreed, and said he could do a lot of the renovations himself. I had my doubts, but I'd chosen the Uxbridge house and felt like it was his turn to choose, plus he made the case that it was within our budget.

So he made up his mind, and that was that.

In the winter of the same year, 1999, my brother Ken bought a cottage on a lake in the Kawarthas, something he'd wanted since our father had sold the family cottage.

His purchase was possible thanks to our Great Aunt Margaret, so once again Ken and I thank our Great Aunt. In the spring, Ken and his family moved into their cottage!

My husband and I moved into our house on Upper Buckhorn Lake on January 22, 1999, on a miserable cold, wet, rainy day. By spring of that year, a complete renovation was underway. First, I had ductwork installed and purchased a new high-energy efficient oil furnace. This was the first thing needed.

I really enjoyed renovating the place. I thought of it as my Special Place, but to renovate it properly, we had to take out a line of credit. I had prefinished oak hardwood floors put in the kitchen and through the dining and living rooms, new white finished cupboards made by Amish carpenters, counter tops in a light pink laminate with black speckles and a light soft peachy pink paint throughout. We also had several new windows added, and a sun room with a laminate floor just off the dining room, with a sliding glass door leading from the sun room to the deck.

The deck overlooked Upper Buckhorn Lake.

We installed a huge steel support bean to allow us to remove two bedrooms and turn the small kitchen into a sunroom, creating one larger room.

The previous owners had not used the house during the winter, flying instead to Florida for the cold months. In spring and fall, they used a wood stove in the basement and a propane fireplace in the living room to provide nominal heat.

This meant that, until we installed the ductwork and furnace in the spring, we froze through the winter months.

When everything was complete, the place looked great. We entertained a lot.

My son asked me if I wanted to babysit my grandson daily, while he and his wife went to work. I declined, because it was important to me that my grandson saw me as his grandmother, not as a babysitter. I would do it occasionally, as needed, but not on a daily basis. That way he and I would appreciate each other and our special relationship.

Like everything in life, there is sometimes too much of a good thing. I think I made the right decision.

Just the same, I did look after my grandson at every opportunity, either at his house or at his Grandma's house on the lake! To this day, he is still my pride and joy. Christmas and holidays mean more because of my grandson, and he never fails to bring joy wherever he goes.

Also in 1999, my ex-husband Ron retired from his job at I.B.M. He was offered another job with a different I.B.M. division that was looking for someone to move to Bermuda and take over a position. Ron accepted, and he and his fiancée moved to Bermuda that year.

~Chapter Fourteen~

In October of 2000, an old high school friend, Maureen, asked me to join her on a trip to Egypt. Her husband didn't want to go, and neither did mine. Not wanting to miss out on such a great opportunity, I traveled with her for twelve days. It was a fantastic experience! We saw an Egyptian museum in Cairo, the pyramids, Giza, the Sphinx, the Catacombs, King Tut's tomb, Alexandria, the Greek-Roman Museum and the Mediterranean Sea.

We saw the forty foot statue of Ramses II and the Alabaster Sphinx, Sakkara's oldest of the pyramids, the Temple of Kings and Queens, Karmuk at night, the light show, Nile Valley, Luxor, the Perfume Factory and a horse-drawn carriage through Edfu to the Temple of Horus.

We sailed on the Nile to Kom Ombo to see the Crocodile and Falcon gods, left for Aswan and saw a turn-of-the-last-century dam, the Temple of Isis, which was transplanted from the submerged island of the Philae.

We saw the granite quarries with an unfinished obelisk. We saw the botanical gardens, boarded a felucca and sailed to the gardens, and yes, we shopped.

I enjoyed a purification massage and a relaxing swim in the pool.

On our last day, we visited Old Cairo and saw Saladin's 12th Century Citadel, the Alabaster Mosque and the Labyrinth Bazaar. We attended a demonstration of how to make papyrus.

The night before we returned home, war broke out in Palestine, and our plane in the northern part of Egypt was delayed. War planes flew overhead. The delay stretched on for a long time, and we were not given any information.

Finally, we were allowed to resume. At the end of that day, our tour guide explained what had happened, and that we would be getting our passports back in the morning. Once we had them, we headed straight to the airport.

To say I was relieved would be an understatement! Every television had images of the fighting. I asked my friend to turn the TV off so I could sleep. Finally, she turned it off.

When we arrived at the airport, there were many soldiers with guns. When we boarded, I was so glad to be headed home.

Travel is marvelous; home is best!

This was almost exactly a year before the 9-11 attack on the New York World Trade Center. If that act of terrorism had happened before our trip, I would not have traveled to Egypt. Our travel agent, oddly, was from the region and had warned us things might be taking a turn for the worse. I'm so glad we traveled when we did, and didn't miss the experience.

I'm a big believer that you should never turn down a good opportunity when it is offered to you. You may never get another chance. So take advantage of every opportunity that presents itself. That is the best way to avoid regrets in life.

Life and time have a way of moving right along.

For the most part, my husband and I enjoyed our beautiful serene home, a quiet place called Emerald Isle, overlooking Upper Buckhorn Lake. We loved watching as the seasons changed. As one season blended into the next, I enjoyed the serenity of living there, and ignored the rearing financial problems, determined to enjoy life.

On April 8, 2001 the phone rang in the early morning. A voice on the other end told me the unexpected news that my ex-husband had died of a massive heart attack in Bermuda.

I was in total shock! Five years earlier, a psychic had told me this would happen. But I'd placed that info onto a back burner in disbelief, mostly because I didn't want to believe it. I stood holding the phone in silence, not knowing what to say or how to say it.

Finally, I asked the caller if I should come down to their place and she said yes. I prepared to go visit the family to see what I could do to help. My husband said he understood.

When I arrived at their house, my emotions felt out of control. I was consumed with depression and disbelief. Even though I'd been divorced from Ron and wasn't in his life anymore, I still felt like a widow. The depth of my feelings shocked me, leaving me feeling raw and strange, to say the least. Apparently, I was unleashing a whirlwind of emotions that I'd kept buried for years.

We were all in a state of grief, the whole family, including Ron's fiancée, although she wasn't there while I was, but instead at her own house.

A couple of days after Ron's death, we were all still feeling the loss acutely, and we decided as a family to walk and picnic down by the lake. My grandson was not quite three years old at the time. We were walking and pushing his carriage when suddenly my little grandson looked up, pointed, and asked, "Who is that bearded man with wings?" We were all dumbfounded, not one of us knew what to say!

Later, my daughter-in-law came downstairs after putting her son to bed. She was half-crying and half-laughing. She told us she'd seen a shadow behind her in her son's room and felt it was Ron. She didn't know how to react.

Over the years, we've had a number of strange occurrences in our family, all unexplained. I'll let you draw your own conclusions. I've already reached my understanding. I'll never forget those strange occurrences, and I cherish them.

My son came to believe, through these strange "events" that there is an afterlife, and the possibility of something beyond the universe as we see it.

The feeling that something, a great and quiet something, exists just beyond our understanding.

Until Ron's death, and these odd appearances, my son did not entertain any belief in an afterlife. So this had a major impact on his beliefs, just as it did on mine.

Ron's death left me shaken. I felt like a breakdown might be coming on. After the funeral, I asked a relative to take me to the psychologist that I used to see.

The psychologist recommended that my husband and I should seek counselling, both together and separately. He warned that, if we didn't take steps to protect our marriage, we would end up in divorce court.

I knew instinctively that the psychologist was right. I'd never properly gotten over the loss of my first marriage. I still loved Ron.

After two weeks, I realized I had to return home to my husband. My family encouraged me to face the reality. I dreaded it, as if I knew what was coming, I just didn't know when.

I'd been away so long that my husband had called and had spoken with my family. From what I could hear of the conversation, it sounded like he'd already decided to leave me, but my relative had talked him out of it, at least for the moment.

Although I did know, on some level, what was happening, I felt like I didn't care, so deep was my grief at Ron's death.

I returned home and tried my best to put on a happy face. I told my husband what the psychologist had recommended, that we seek counselling as a couple. He, of course, did not believe me and we did not go for help.

Looking back, I realize I might as well have left him then, for all the good my efforts did.

A year later, almost to the day, in April of 2002, the phone rang with bad news again. This time, the voice told me that a very close family member had attempted suicide. He'd been in Florida, and had tried to slice his wrists, but something forced him to stop and call 911.

Thank God Almighty, he did stop, and he did call 911.

I tried my best to get myself together to drive down and see if I could help in any way. For some reason, I couldn't pull myself together. I was in shock, in fact dumbfounded, although on the outside I know I looked calm and collected.

My family member finally called to say that my relative had driven to Florida without me. Given my state of mind at the time, it was probably for the best. I may not have been any help under the circumstances.

Once my relatives returned to Canada, I immediately drove to the hospital to see them.

It took some effort and arguing, but we finally convinced staff at the hospital that they had to admit our relative, for his own safety. That's when I learned that my youngest relative had been obsessively drinking, using cocaine and not taking care of himself.

My dear relative had become an addict.

I discovered the awful truth, that at the age of five, my relative had been abused by a babysitter. I was shocked! For years he'd blocked out the memories, believing he had imagined them, until eventually the truth all came crashing down on him.

We convinced him to enter rehab for help. My husband suggested our relative should come and live with us. I was so relieved that I didn't have to ask him. After a few months, my young relative came to live with my husband and me at the lake.

It turned out to be a difficult arrangement. We had no experience in how to handle this situation.

Before long, we put the lake house up for sale. We really could not afford it, and besides, I wanted to be closer to hospitals and rehab for my relative's sake.

In July of 2002 we bought a house and moved to Cobourg. My husband got a transfer to Port Hope, and Cobourg was very close to there.

I found a beautiful brick custom-built house with a two-car garage and a finished basement. We rented out the lower level to help with the mortgage. We'd been searching for a new place for a long time, the whole while my husband was trying to convince me to move to Port Hope. I refused, because Port Hope is the only place in Ontario where the soil has to be checked regularly for radiation.

Of course, my hesitation might have been my own doubts playing out, a little voice telling me not to buy another house with this man.

In the end, we went to look at the place in Cobourg. We bought it.

My husband insisted that we divide the rent money equally between us, even though he had a paying job and I was paying far more than my share of the mortgage. With him, everything was about money. At least, that's the way he made me feel.

It was a very large house. The finished basement had two bedrooms, a full bathroom, and a kitchen, and there was a shared laundry room on the main floor.

Also on the main floor, we had a dining room, living room, den, kitchen and a two piece bathroom. There was a wrap-around deck off the kitchen and front entrance.

Upstairs were three more bedrooms and two full bathrooms. You entered the basement through the shared laundry room on the main level.

I don't remember how much we charged for rent once we became landlords. I only remember how angry I became over his insistence that we share the rent, even though my condo equity had been used to purchase both places and I carried more than my share of the mortgage. Looking back, I don't know why I agreed. I think I just had too much on my plate at the time, and wanted to keep the peace.

Knowing now that he was already planning to leave me, I wish I'd fought harder.

But at the time, everything felt overwhelming, and he was also driving me crazy with his demands.

My young relative went to A.A. meetings. I made sure I took him. I made a commitment to learn where and when meetings took place, and also drove him to Toronto weekly for his rehab meetings. I also attended a meeting for families of people with addictions.

No one else in the family was willing to go, and they all had their own family obligations. As the mother, it was right that I should go, but it would have been nice to have some family support.

My second husband was completely unwilling to attend. I became obsessed with keeping an eye on my family member, trying to make sure he was safe and that his behaviour was under control.

One Friday night, after we had moved to Cobourg, my young relative left the house by taxi and headed for a drinking and drug binge in Toronto.

In every meeting I'd attended, they'd emphasized the need to say what you mean and mean what you say. They recommended tough love, consistency.

I had warned my relative that if he started back in on drinking and drugs, he would have to leave my house.

After the weekend, he called to ask if he could come home. I told him I'd have to think about it and asked him to call me the next day.

When he called again I had to make one of the hardest decisions of my lifetime. I told him he could not come back, that he would have to get help and stay clean.

My first husband had spoiled him, and he'd always gotten his way on everything, which I believed was part of the problem. I knew I would have to be strong.

After throwing my young relative out, I sank into a depression. I was convinced that, any day, a police officer was going to call me to say my relative had taken his own life, or had died. I prayed every night before bed, asking my Higher Power to keep him safe and guide him. I also repeated the Serenity prayer every night.

A year later, in January 2004, he called to ask if he could visit for a few days. He told me he was ready to make a change. I wanted to believe it.

When he arrived at my door, I saw the shell of a man he had become. His head was a skull and you could see the bones in his face. I made up the sofa for him to sleep.

The next day we talked. I told him about a place in Guelph that I thought might be able to help him with his abuse and addiction. He said he would go. I put him on a train. He went to the place in Guelph, and he said it helped him.

Meanwhile, my second husband was acting like a baby, saying I should have asked his permission before allowing my relative to stay a few days. Since I was paying more than my share, it was my home too, and I didn't feel I needed permission to open my doors to a close relative in need.

Needless to say, I didn't need this nonsense in my life. I was stressed enough, without him giving me grief. And I couldn't believe the complaint he was coming up with. It seemed too ridiculous for words.

By February of 2004, my second husband informed me he wanted a divorce. He said it had nothing to do with my family member, instead it was a number of things, most of which did not make sense to me. He complained that I'd never loved him. I didn't argue. I told him I did love him. But I was exhausted from everything I'd been through, and didn't have the strength to argue.

He was not willing to go for counselling, so that was that.

One of his complaints was that I never took him out to dinner, or did any of the driving when we went out. I discussed this with a family member, who asked me what I planned to do about it. So after thinking about it, I decided to make reservations for Valentine's Day at a fancy restaurant in Cobourg. I bought a sexy nightgown and took him out, driving to give him a break.

We ended up having sex, which was very painful for me, both physically and emotionally. But I felt I needed to keep this marriage going.

Afterwards, he asked me why I'd had sex with him. I answered, truthfully, to try to keep the marriage going. He said, "Well, it's over."

I felt humiliated for having tried, and it made no difference, his mind had been made up all along. I felt devastated, like a total failure.

But looking back, I see that he did me a favour. There had been so many clues, so many times when I thought I should leave, but I hadn't wanted to give in.

I'd even been told by a professional that the marriage was in trouble, but I hadn't listened.

For some time, he'd been erratic in his behaviour and difficult to live with, making it hard to carry on a regular routine or just to live each day.

Still, to say I was surprised was an understatement.

I got a job at a resort in Roseneath, Ontario, cleaning cottages and washing windows. In early March, the snow had not gone yet, and it was cold, damp work. I came home one day, exhausted and frozen from a day spent washing windows out in the cold. Even though we worked in groups of women, the job was brutal.

When I got home, my husband showed no sympathy and was being a bastard. I went to bed and tried to stop shivering. I ended up sick after that.

They even had us painting outside, which was not part of our job. I ended up injuring myself and had to go for physiotherapy, and on Workers' Compensation.

My last day of work was May 17, 2004. The resort said I would be welcome back to work any time. But I had to pack up my house and put it onto the market. What my employer didn't know was that I would be moving as soon as the house was sold.

My mind was a blur from the strain of living with an individual who was no longer reasonable, but up and down like a yo-yo. I could never predict what he would do next. After dealing with the addiction issues of my young relative, the behaviour of my husband was simply too much. I was exhausted.

I wanted to run away, to just get out of there, but my lawyer said no, I would have to stay to ensure I didn't get robbed of my equity in the house. I could not allow him to drive me out of my house. It was like walking on a tight rope.

~Chapter Fifteen~

By the time we sold the house, it had been exactly two years since we'd moved in.

My young relative and I moved to Ajax. My ex moved to Oshawa where he had bought a house.

I was so scared and exhausted throughout the failure of this marriage that I wanted to lay down and die, but something propelled me forward. There was so much to do, and I couldn't give in to depression.

After we moved, I didn't miss my husband at all. He was like a huge weight that I could finally drop.

We moved to Ajax and stayed with another family member for a couple of weeks, then rented a one-bedroom basement apartment. My belongings were on a storage truck in Port Hope until I could land a job and a permanent home to buy. I tried out for a job at Minacs on November 27, 2004. It was a telephone switch board operator trial. I was there until December, but didn't get the job.

I did get a job at Winners and after three months, bought a Power of Sale townhouse in the south part of Ajax. My young relative was in bad shape from all of the stress, but eventually he became healthy and got his strength back. He began helping me by working and fixing my townhouse up. He also attended regular meetings, got himself a sponsor, then another sponsor, with whom he really clicked.

I was no longer nagging him to go to meetings. He was going on his own initiative. I was exhausted and finally realized I couldn't and shouldn't try to control everything. It was much better for him to want to go to meetings.

My young family member could see I was unhappy. He pointed out that I seemed to have anger issues of my own. He suggested that I should try attending Al-Anon.

I didn't think it would help, but he asked, "What do you have to lose?"

So, one warm summer evening, I decided to give it a try. I went off to a meeting. To my surprise, it did help. I discovered a sense of calmness. I'd never realized that people actually cared, and shared many of the same problems. We were there to support each other, and to take our focus off the addicts in our lives.

Al-Anon is a program designed to help the families of addicts and alcoholics. The program continues to help me, and I was also able to give back, to know the happiness of helping others with the same problems. My anxiety finally went away, and I found a calmness and contentment I had never known before.

This program helped me to focus on myself, and not on my family member, which is critical both for my own well-being and for his.

I'd like to acknowledge the Al-Anon program and the fellowship I found there for all the help and changes it brought to my life, at a time when I really needed help.

"As long as you live, keep learning how to live." Seneca, from Courage to Change, page 240. This passage seems to sum up what I feel about moving forward, and not living in the past.

My young relative has been clean and sober since 2007. He held down a full time job, and in 2008 he moved out and got his own apartment.

Before moving out, he was involved in a terrible accident. He was almost killed. He was trying to help a neighbour. He was between two parked cars, helping his neighbour by holding the car, when his neighbour took his foot off the brake and forgot to put the clutch in place. The car rolled back and crushed my relative. It's a miracle that he lived and that he can function normally. He did recover. He uses acupuncture to control the pain and enjoys a full life.

After five years working part time with the City, he was employed full time. In 2009, my prayers for him were answered, when he met and married a woman in November 2009. I was concerned that he hadn't known her long, but he was determined.

I developed shingles. I'd worn myself out looking after my ailing Dad, and now this surprise wedding! What doesn't kill you makes you stronger, and I must be made of steel by now!

In November, 2008, I was officially divorced from my second husband, but not without a fight for his benefits. He didn't want to give them to me, but after two court visits he realized I was not going to give in, so he made this concession.

Also, he paid for the divorce.

He would not agree to alimony, but since it would have been a minimal amount, I let it go. It wasn't worth the struggle.

It definitely pays to stick up for your rights!

Much later, after our divorce was final, I had my engagement ring refurbished into hoop earrings. That way I could get some use of them, without having to see them and thinking of the past.

On August 16, 2008, my father was about to turn the ripe old age of 90. I decided to call and arrange to see him. We set a date. Lo and behold, Teivel was there, but thankfully she was asleep. Other times, when I'd visited, she'd been awake and had created a scene, yelling at me to get out. After that, we usually would meet at a coffee shop across the street from his apartment.

I asked my father if he would like to meet his great grandson.

He agreed, and asked them to meet him in the lobby.

So we made a plan: my daughter-in-law would bring her son. When they arrived, Dad said he had given Teivel a sleeping pill, and they could come up for a visit.

So up they went, and had a nice visit. My dad was thrilled to meet his 10-year-old great grandson for the first time.

As my father's birthday drew closer, I asked him if I could bring him a cake and pizza. He said yes. To my surprise, Teivel's daughter had sent her to a hospital due to bedsores and not eating properly. Her daughter was trying to get Teivel into a nursing home.

My father called me and told me exactly when Teivel would be out with her daughter. On August 16, 2008, I brought him his cake and pizza and two documents from the Canadian government congratulating my father on his 90th birthday!

He was thrilled, but he was also worn out from caring for Teivel. It was too much for anyone to do on their own, much less a man of 90 years.

I asked my dad if he would like me to look after him. He said he would like that. I told him I had a few things to do first, so he stayed at my place for one night, but the stairs were too hard on him.

I realized the best solution would be for me to move in with him. But first, I had to obtain a Power of Attorney for his health as well as his finances. This was on the suggestion of a trusted friend.

I moved in with Dad on December 1, 2008. Part of me was hesitant, but another part was anxious for the chance to get to know my dad again before it was too late.

I didn't realize how much stress the move and caring for Dad would add to my life. I was already working at two jobs. It became too much. I developed a case of shingles on the night of my son's wedding, but didn't realize it till a couple of days later when I visited my doctor.

I became a landlady again in 2008-2009, renting out my townhouse. However, the lady I rented to started to trash my house, so I evicted her and sold the house. I invested the money, to keep it safe for when I was ready to buy again.

When I first moved in with my father, I was surprised by the neighbours in his building constantly asking me why he "took it". When I asked what they meant, they said that living with Teivel must have been hell for him, the way she fought constantly and yelled at my father. They couldn't understand why he put up with it.

My guess was that he was trapped in an abusive relationship and didn't have the skills to recognize it. Also, his deep religion would have caused him to stay no matter how hard it was.

Sometimes, when we are in the thick of that kind of relationship, we can't see the forest for the trees. We just struggle on, trying to survive each day, and not seeing the bigger picture, like how much happier we would be without the abuser.

By the time I'd moved in with my father, my young relative was already on his own, following his own guiding plan. I also had a plan to follow, and it involved "minding my own business" and allowing him to get on with his improved life.

Those are the words I try to live by now: Mind your own business.

I follow the wisdom of the Serenity Prayer:

> *God, grant me the serenity to accept the things I cannot change,*
> *The courage to change the things I can,*
> *And the wisdom to know the difference.*

I don't know where my life would be today without this prayer. It has truly saved me.

Everything that has happened in my life has been for a reason, this I know. But in truth, I haven't always understood the reason. Some things are simply beyond my control and beyond my understanding.

That is what I remind myself daily. It's important to learn to let go, to not try to control those things you cannot. Otherwise, you'll drive yourself crazy.

In May 2009, my eldest family member and his family were headed back to Bermuda for a visit. I asked if I could join them. I really needed a break.

They said yes. I had enough Air Miles to pay for my flight both ways.

We rented a cottage and brought a lot of canned food with us. There was also a grocery store near our rental place. On Sundays, they put their inventory on sale, so we stocked up on enough food to last the week. Bermuda tends to be a very expensive place to shop.

I felt so fortunate to be allowed to tag along with them. It was a dream come true! Bermuda was a place I'd always wanted to see, but would never have gone to on my own. And I'll probably never go again.

I hired someone to look after my dad for a week, but it was worth it! I even rode a scooter while we were there. The sand is pink, candy for the eyes.

We visited the house where Ron had lived during his time in Bermuda. I couldn't bring myself to go inside. We visited Ron's favourite beach, went to an aquarium, saw a fort general walking all over the town of Hamilton and traveled to many places by bus. But as usual, in the blink of an eye, our vacation was over! Before we knew it, we were back on the tarmac, boarding a plane to return home.

The Orr Lake property I mentioned earlier had been in my family since 1896. When my great aunt Margaret Barclay was born, her grandfather Christopher Nixon purchased the lake property. On his death in 1913, it was passed to his daughter, Maria Louisa (Nixon) Barclay. Maria didn't know what to do with the property, so she passed it to her daughter, my great-aunt Margaret.

Great Aunt Margaret had given a lot to my father for his 21st birthday.

The waterfront lot was quite large, at least 150 X 100. It was on a small spring fed lake close to Toronto, between Elmvale and Hillsdale, off Highway 93 near Wasaga Beach. It was a sandy, shallow lake that you could walk into for a great distance before you reached any significant depth.

The north side of the lake was weedy, but not Aunt Margaret's cottage, which was on the south side.

When I was a small child, my father sold half the property to another family. He sold the other half of the property in 1971, after he married Teivel. That ended his possession of the lot Aunt Margaret had given him.

I do remember trying very hard to convince Dad not to sell the property, but he insisted that he had to. Years later, I learned he sold it to purchase a new car. When I told him he should have applied for a loan, instead of selling, he replied that he hadn't thought of that. He also said he regretted selling the property. I told him I also regretted it!

Dad also insisted we could not take anything out of the cottage, because the new owners had purchased it lock, stock and barrel. I decided that was bologna, and when my brother mentioned he wanted Dad's RCAF propeller that had hung in the cottage, I told him to go ahead and take it. I also gave him Dad's RCAF shaving mug, and I took a bread knife that Dad had put a new handle on.

We never told Dad we took these things, but it was lucky we did. One day, when we were visiting our great aunt's cottage, we passed the place Dad had sold and saw several of those cherished items out on the street for garbage pickup. There was a beautiful old spindle chair, a medicine cabinet, an ice box, among the things we would have cherished but were forbidden to take.

One day shortly after Dad sold the cottage, Ron and I were driving north in our robin-egg blue Volkswagen Beetle. Our car was so small we could not even pick up these items from the side of the road.

So I was glad I'd insisted my brother take the WWII wooden propeller he'd wanted. Seeing those beloved memories sitting at the side of the road and not being able to claim them was a very painful thing.

I was disappointed in my father, knowing he cared so little about our family memories that he could just sell everything off with the cottage. It's a hard thing for me to admit, but it wasn't all Teivel's fault. It's been really hard for me to come to terms with my father's flaws, but I realize it had a lot to do with the way he was raised.

Keep in mind, he pretty much raised himself. Most of his decisions were based on momentary needs, and not on what would be best in the long term. With no parental guidance, he had no knowledge of what to compare his decisions to.

At least this is what I now tell myself.

Years later, when he told me of his regrets about selling the cottage, it did help me a great deal with my own sense of loss. It helped me to understand, and to feel less alone in my own regrets.

The new owners were a family who had rented our cottage for years. After buying it, they tore it down and built a big beautiful home in its place.

My heart was broken over the sale of that cottage, that little brick insole container of my best memories. I'd loved the lake, and many of my childhood memories were not great, but being at Orr Lake made up the best of those memories.

After Dad sold the cottage, I felt like I was losing my mother all over again, my memories of her and of our time as a family had been sold, torn down and replaced by a different family.

Even during my mother's illness, when she couldn't come north as often, I still loved the memories of being there with her. Family dinners, entertaining friends, family reunions.

Then, later, memories of Ron and me when we first started dating – those memories remain precious to me.

Nothing can ever bring those times back. I weep even these days for the long lost property and the happy times that I will never get back.

I hope I've been able to help you, my reader, understand why losing this property meant so much to me. Later, the sadness was compounded by the selling of

Aunt Margaret's larger, fully winterized home on Orr Lake.

A house is only a house. This is what we tell ourselves. But in my experience, place provides us with a sense of continuity that nothing else can give us.

After losing these places, I felt all alone, even though Ron and I were still married. I see now that I was not in good shape. I was a very immature young woman, still a child in many ways. And losing my mother, followed by losing these places I held so dear, made everything seem so much worse.

After I was discharged from the hospital, my psychiatrist told me I'd spent a lot of time pacing back and forth on the street with the baby carriage. He said that kind of pacing was the kind a cat will do when it's searching for its mother. He believed it was a sign of how much I missed my mother, and that had led to my breakdown after having the baby. I always remember his words, and they made sense to me.

Ron was also very young, and my breakdown was a lot for him to deal with. But he did stick by me, and his mother also helped a lot, looking after our first son until I was well enough to do it myself in 1971.

It certainly wasn't what I had imagined, for my first few years of marriage!

Whenever my father visited, he preached at us about the New World. He insisted our world was close to ending and that I needed to return to JW meetings. Neither he nor his so-called Christian wife Teivel offered me any practical help at all, only Ron and his mother did that.

I always resented how little my father helped, but I remain grateful to this day for what Ron and my mother-in-law Mina did when I needed help.

My intuition about Teivel proved to be spot on. She married my father for a meal ticket. He paid for everything in their marriage, and also gave his money to her and to her children and grandchild. She controlled my father in every possible way. She took over his life like a vulture, controlling his bank accounts and every aspect of his day. It was in no way a fair or equal relationship.

Dad just signed the cheques whenever she demanded.

Whatever relationship I'd had with my father until that point deteriorated quickly after Teivel came into the picture. Between his wife and his religion, there was nothing left for me, for my brother or for our families.

I can easily count the number of times Dad had any significant part in our lives after he married Teivel. His own wedding day. The births of my two children. The day I introduced my Dad to his father. The one and only weekend he spent looking after my children. My brother's wedding in 1978. My Dad's retirement from the post office in 1983, when I took him out for a drink to celebrate.

By my calculation, that is a total of seven times I had contact with my father, from the time they were married until just before Teivel was put into a nursing home, because her own family could not handle her and the neighbours were complaining about her yelling and screaming.

When our children were little, Ron and I spent a lot of Christmases at our home with my brother Ken, and his wife and children. Later, we took turns, spending some Christmases at Ken's house, which was a great help. Of course, my brother's children were younger than ours, so it made sense to be at their house alternately.

I now realize that I did way too much back then to decorate, to create a "picture-perfect" holiday home. It seems I had a tendency to become obsessed, to need everything in the house to be perfect over the holidays.

The result was that I wore myself out. By the time Christmas dinner rolled around, I could hardly enjoy it, I was so exhausted.

And other people really don't appreciate it fully. They don't feel the need for decoration the way I felt it. One of my family members likes to decorate, but the other can't be bothered, and neither of their wives are into it.

I find it disconcerting that they pay so little attention, but it's not the end of the world. I've come to realize that to each his own, as the saying goes. Besides, I'm pretty sure my own obsession with post-card Christmases stems from the fact that we never celebrated the holidays when I was growing up. I always felt left out, like I was missing something truly important, the traditions of Christmas, Easter, and Thanksgiving that all my school mates enjoyed.

I longed for that kind of home as a child! I'm sure that's what drove me to overdo my own efforts as an adult.

It was only when Teivel was finally put into a nursing home by her daughter that I was able to restore my relationship with my father. I arranged for him to call me as soon as she was secured in a home, and then I brought him cake and pizza for his 90th birthday.

We enjoyed our little celebration, and I was able to show him the acknowledgements of his 90th birthday from the government of Canada. He really liked that!

I hated all the sneaking around that was necessary, just to build some kind of relationship with my own father. That was unforgiveable as far as I was concerned. It wasn't like we were doing anything wrong! I was his daughter, for Pete's sake. It should have been natural for us to spend quality time together, but Teivel had created such a wedge between us, it's a miracle we were finally able to get past it.

But the controlling attitudes of Teivel and her family made it necessary for us to deceive them in order to spend time together. It also fuelled my desire to protect him, to help him stay one step ahead of their manipulative ways.

There is a well-known expression: Where there is a will, there is a way.

That has been my experience throughout my life, and I also believe that God works in mysterious ways at times.

After 37 years apart, it was bittersweet being reunited, because Dad was no longer the man he'd been when I was young. He had a mild case of dementia, something I was not aware of when I'd agreed to move in and care for him.

Of course, that wasn't surprising given his age. And he did need my help. His condo was cluttered and dirty, full of expired food and mess. When I arrived, he had been still trying to cook and eat expired food. I had to stop him and buy new food.

Dad had been declared incompetent to drive his car in 2006, and yet he was continuing to drive in 2008. Just before I moved in, he had another car accident. I contacted his neurologist, who informed me she'd sent a letter of incompetence to the Ministry, but for some reason they had not received it and had not revoked his licence.

In February of 2009, Dad went out driving. He became confused and didn't know where he was. I stopped him from driving after that, and that's when I learned about his incompetence.

While Teivel had been living in the condo with my father, Ken and I had not been allowed to visit. But Teivel's family had been there often, running errands for her and looking after her. They did not pay any attention to Dad, simply neglected him and left his well-being by the wayside.

When my father's dementia became obvious, he could not remember visiting the neurologist at all. I had to keep the truth about his dementia away from Teivel and her family, as I couldn't trust them. Teivel had always used her JW religion as an excuse to keep Ken and me from seeing our father.

In my opinion, Teivel had used my father as her personal gopher from the day she married him. He was her bank account, her errand boy and her whipping post. She never treated him well. She was a hypocrite and a hypochondriac, using her imaginary illnesses to manipulate him.

From what I witnessed, she never showed any kindness or gratitude to my father. She never had a kind word for anyone. I've never before met anyone quite like Teivel, and I hope I never do again.

After I'd been looking after Dad for a while, I finally got the courage to ask him why he'd stayed in that relationship.

He said he'd believed he had no choice. He was the husband, and he never considered leaving.

My father, Jack didn't realize he was in an abusive relationship, but I firmly believe that's exactly what it was. She isolated him from his family, which is a classic symptom of abuse. And religion was her primary weapon.

~Chapter Sixteen~

For the next three years, from December 1, 2008 until he passed away on February 12, 2012, I looked after my Dad. I gained a new insight into his life, gained tolerance form him, empathy and even some sympathy. I learned to put myself into his shoes, and to gain a new perspective on what his life had been like, how he had suffered living and dealing with his second wife and her family.

I understand now that there are many reasons people do the things they do. As much as I hate to admit it, life is full of grey areas. Not everything is black or white.

Thank heavens I was able to enjoy those years, to love my father and to be open enough to see the reasons behind his decisions and actions for what they were.

I'm reminded over and over there are so many things in life that are beyond our understanding. In the end, if we can accept that and not dwell on it we'll be much better off. This knowledge has helped to make my life more complete and satisfied, and it was my honour to be able to help my father and to bring our family back together in some small way.

No one can know everything, especially not me! But there are many ways to accomplish the things we want to achieve. We just have to be determined and look for the ways, and always try to make a difference. We need to try to understand what we can, try to be a good person. I'll never regret helping my father. It made me stronger, and it made me a better person.

Due to his dementia, my father was losing control of his finances. He was falling into a habit of buying everything that was promoted to him through the mail. This is a common problem with the elderly.

There was an upside to my father's compulsive shopping: Teivel and her family had not been able to stop him either! That meant they were not able, in the end, to get their hands on the rest of his money. That was a kind of poetic justice, in my opinion.

One day I came home from work and asked Dad if there had been any mail. He proceeded to tell me about a promotion where, if he made a purchase of $39.99, he'd receive $70,000.00!

I told him it was a scam, but he didn't believe me. I was so frustrated and exhausted that I decided to call the police and tell them about the scam.

They asked me to fax the paperwork over to them, and call them the next day. When I called them the next day, the officer instructed me to remove my father's credit cards from him. It was obvious to the police that my father had become a victim of people who prey on the elderly.

My father was not happy losing his cards, but it had to be done.

I hated exerting this control over my father. In my view, he'd been under Teivel's control for so many years, it just seemed so unfair, now that he was free, to have to take away his control once again. But it couldn't be helped. His dementia was already stealing his control over his actions, and the responsibility to correct the situation was on me. I'd agreed to care for my Dad. Part of that care was making sure he was not victimized in this way.

When I'd moved in, I'd falsely assumed my Dad was still in control of his faculties. I had thought we'd rebuild a friendship, that he'd do his thing, I'd do mine, and I'd care for him and we'd have time together at the end of the day.

Thanks to his dementia, I got a lot more than I'd bargained for!

Unbeknownst to me, Dad also had diabetes. On December 1, 2008, I called the Veterans' office and learned he qualified for a small pension. They also had an adult Day program. Initially, I enrolled Dad to visit the program one day per week, but we soon increased it to three days per week, because Dad really enjoyed the social aspect and the activities. He also really liked the lunch they provided.

They also were able to help me out a lot with car rides to doctors' appointments for Dad, diabetic Meals on Wheels and some of his care.

When it finally became too much for me on my own, I was able to get him into a Veterans' nursing home, the Tony Stacey Centre. At the end, Dad's case was considered a crisis situation and they managed to fast-track him into a placement.

I was truly grateful for all of this help in caring for Dad. It came down to me making a single phone call. All I had to do was to reach out. And I honestly don't believe I would have been able to manage everything without their help.

The Veterans' office was so well organized. When I called them, they asked for Dad's enlistment number. He'd been in the Royal Canadian Air Force during WWII. I located his enlistment papers, and found a letter he'd written to his own Aunt Kit, as he was preparing to join the Air Force.

I will treasure these papers, and keep them as a reference of his life.

My Dad was so very pleased and grateful for all the help we were given by the Veterans' office. The Jehovah's Witnesses would have discouraged him from asking them for help, as they were against anything related to war. Luckily, his fellow-JWs knew nothing about it and I was able to keep it hidden from Teivel and her family.

There was one other thing I was determined to put right, to make up for the way Teivel had treated my father. I contacted the Canadian Post Office, where my Dad had worked his whole life, and I explained to them what his abusive wife had made him do. Teivel, if you'll recall, had forced Dad to return the retirement gift of a watch he'd received for 37 years of service earlier in 1983.

The lady I spoke with was very understanding. She told me they could not replace the exact watch they had given him, as it was now obsolete. However, she said they could give him an ordinary watch with a special strap and pins to represent his time at the Post Office. I was delighted!

When I told my father about this, he was really pleased and could hardly believe it!

As for me, I felt I had righted a wrong that had been done to my Dad and our family.

I was so very grateful for their help. In the end, Teivel did not get away entirely with those years of belittling Dad and making him feel that nothing he did was important. The fact the Post Office would help and honour Dad in this way restored my faith in the kindness of people.

Given the history of my relationship with Dad, I never would have guessed I'd have the chance to care for him in his old age. It makes me feel there really is some kind of destiny, over which we have no control. I'd been very concerned about my own ability to properly care for Dad, especially as each new health wrinkle was discovered and given the truth about our past lack of relationship.

But it ended up being a truly healing and satisfying venture for me. I believe I became a better person, and I accomplished so much more than I ever thought possible.

Dad was happy during that time, and he was grateful I'd stepped up to the plate.

At some point, I discovered Dad had a picture of his parents that he kept hidden in his wallet. I found that sweet, but also very sad, since they had not been together long, and he'd had very little relationship with his mother, and none at all with his father.

I've included that sad, sweet photo in this book, and I hope you'll study it and see the sweetness I see there.

I think Dad's Aunt Margaret must have given him that photo, because she was present at that wedding, and it was her handwriting on the back of the photo.

There was another thing I managed to correct while caring for Dad. In the family section of the cemetery, Aunt Margaret had purchased memorial stones for all family members. However she'd made a mistake when she ordered Dad's stone. Instead of putting his proper name of Jack Telford Denis Sharpe, she had inadvertently put John Barclay Sharpe. Many people who use the name Jack are properly named John, but that was not the case with Dad. This mistake always bothered him.

When I learned about this, I asked him if he would like me to have the stone corrected. He said yes, so that I did. I felt this was a huge accomplishment, something seemingly small that made him very happy, so he would know he would be marked properly when he passed into eternity.

This is something that never would have happened if I'd not been there with him at the end. There was no one else who cared about what was important to my Dad, only me. So it was something I could give him that no one else would. And I was happy to do it.

While I was at it, I also added my mother's name and my name as well as my brother's, my paternal grandparents' and my father's sister, and I had a photo of my father and mother added to the stone. The effect was truly beautiful, and Dad was pleased.

In spite of the treatment he'd received from Teivel for all those years, in the end he was not alone. Our relationship endured. I was so glad I've never completely written him off during those years, that I'd done my best to keep up some minimal contact.

I have no regrets, only a contentment and sense of satisfaction over what I was able to accomplish in restoring that vital relationship. For this opportunity, I am grateful, and thankful.

There was a definite sense of healing throughout my family. My niece went to visit my Dad in the hospital, and so did my brother, Ken. When Dad could clearly no longer drive his car, Ken helped me to sell it.

My eldest niece told me what had changed her mind about going to visit her grandfather. At first, she hadn't wanted to go. But she paid attention to something I had said about abusive relationships. She understood that, if she didn't make the effort to see him, his abuser would win.

That thought stopped her in her tracks, and made her re-think the entire thing.

So, because I asked them to, my nieces, my two sons and their wives, all met my father at last. He also got to meet his great grandson, which would not have happened if I had not pressed for it.

In February of 2009, a first cousin of Ron's passed away of a rare disease at the age of 61. She is sadly missed by our family. You know how, when you meet certain people, you just connect? Well, she was like that, very down-to-earth. I hope there is an afterlife, so I can see her again. Missing her breaks my heart. I refuse to think I'll never see her again.

I know it was a Higher Power that gave me the strength to care for my father when he needed me most. I also give a lot of credit to Al-Anon, as their principles helped me to change the way I thought, and to live in a more positive way. Al-Anon is not a religious group, it's a group to help families of addicts. The principles they teach are helpful in many family situations, not just those effected by alcohol and drug abuse.

Before I discovered Al-Anon, I pushed God out of my life. Being raised in such a strict religious sect, and so closed off from the rest of the world, made me determined not to give anyone control over my life.

I'd had enough of religion, especially one whose members seemed totally self-absorbed, and who had completely rejected my brother and myself. We had been Dis-fellowshipped. We were not allowed to attend Kingdom Hall, and were not allowed to associate with JW members.

This is the excuse Teivel was able to use to isolate Ken and me from our father.

Of course, my father carries most of the blame. After all, he was a grown man and made his own decisions. This was the thing I found most difficult to deal with, during the time I spent caring for him. Through his own actions and decisions, he'd chosen to favour his abuser over his own children.

When I was making the decision to move in with Dad and care for him, I wasn't at all sure I could do it. I was still bitter, and could not understand how or why he had shut us out for all those years. Many questions went through my head. Basically, my worst nightmare was coming to pass: I was being asked to forgive the man who had betrayed me and my brother, and more than forgive him, I was being asked to turn the other cheek and care for him.

When I entered Dad's condo, everything there reminded me of his wife, Teivel. It was stressful, to say the least.

That's why I know I could not have done it without help. After everything that had happened between us, it would have been incomprehensible.

But looking back, I'm so very happy for the decisions I made. The rewards far out-weighed the transgressions of the past.

Finally, after some time had passed, I opened up to Dad about my opinion of Teivel. I told him I didn't trust her to be honest. I told him exactly what I thought of her.

Teivel was more concerned with money than anything else. Even recently, she was still yelling about the fact that Dad and she did not get the bulk of the inheritance from my great-aunt Margaret. At that time, in 2009, Teivel had a bladder infection and was in the hospital. I was caring for Dad and a family member drove him to the hospital to visit her. But I learned she'd been screaming at him in the hospital, deriding him because in 1987 his Aunt Margaret had not left him all her money.

Finally, a family member brought Dad home to his condo, as he was distraught and embarrassed over her abusive behaviour. Even in a hospital bed, Teivel had the power and the desire to abuse my father.

When he returned home and told me about the situation, I was furious. For a religion that supposedly doesn't place importance on money, Teivel spent all of her waking time talking and thinking about how she could get her hands on more. It wasn't even her money to worry about. Aunt Margaret had done what she thought was best. She hadn't wanted Teivel to grab all of her inheritance. Thank goodness Aunt Margaret could see what type of person Teivel was.

I was so angry, I told my father that Teivel was a money-grabbing witch.

Looking back, I can see that Teivel suffered from mental problems. At one point, she had attempted suicide, and other members of her family had committed suicide. There were inherent mental issues for sure.

Teivel's entire family had belonged to the Jehovah's Witnesses. JWs do not believe in psychologists or psychiatrists, and I really don't understand that belief set. In my opinion, every single person can use help from all types of health care, at one point or another in their lives.

Whether medical, naturopathic or psychological, we all need help for our minds, bodies and spirits. The psychological profession helped me a great deal, and maybe if Teivel's family members had looked for help, they might still be alive.

My father got stuck in a marriage from hell and didn't know how to get out, or thought it was his duty to stay.

That's another thing the JWs do: they discourage divorce, saying the only justification for leaving a marriage is adultery or death. So if things don't work out, tough! You're trapped in the situation, no matter how bad it is. That makes no sense at all to me!

Jack never thought to check into what Teivel was doing with his money. By the time I started looking into it, it was too late. He'd already spent a lifetime with a woman who'd robbed him blind. She spent it on herself and her family, giving them large amounts.

I discovered Dad had also been making large annual donations to the JW religion. That religion had another kind of control over my father. So long as they got his annual donation, they didn't care about the state of his life or his marriage. Teivel was a good actress, pretending to be the good wife whenever their JW friends visited.

As I began my own detective work, I spoke to many of their neighbours. It's amazing what you can find out.

My father would never talk to me or Ken about the way Teivel treated him. He wouldn't open up to his friends, or even his church about the abuse. He was in denial.

There was an incident when she went after him with a knife and he was forced to lock himself in a bathroom to get away from her. To this day, the bathroom door still has knife marks, and he carried scars on his arms that frankly looked like knife marks.

Another time, I was tired, angry and frustrated while talking with him. I raised my arms in frustration, and he winced, sure I was going to hit him. Of course I'd had no intention of hitting him. But it made me wonder what he had really suffered at the hands of his abusive wife.

There are no good words I can find for Teivel. She normally put up a good front in the company of friends and strangers. But there was one time, when Dad was 89 years old, I was visiting him and her care worker was bathing her. Teivel went crazy, screaming at me to get out of the condo, even though I wasn't doing anything, just visiting my father quietly. She couldn't stand to have anyone else in his life. She became so agitated that her care worker was afraid she would have a coronary and so she asked me to leave.

Until that point, there had been so few times I'd seen my father. He didn't want me to leave, and tried to stick up for himself and for me.

But in the end, I left and told Dad we'd have to meet outside of the condo in future. He agreed.

I bit my tongue for far too long, but everyone has a boiling point, and eventually I did tell Dad exactly what I thought of his wife. But that was when I was caring for him.

I hope God has a different plan in mind for Teivel, so we won't have to see her in heaven. Hopefully, a plan that matches the way she treated Dad and our family.

If I'm forced to find one good thing about his marriage to Teivel, I'd say it was that he did manage to travel a fair bit and see the world. Of course, if he hadn't married her he probably still would have traveled, and my family and I would have gone with him.

No discussion of Teivel would be complete without describing her terrible, shrieking yell! I've never heard anything like it in my life. It was a blood-curdling scream, like you would imagine coming out of the mouth of a witch in a scary movie. I promise I'm not exaggerating, that's exactly what she sounded like. She had this terrifying voice and a terrible temperament to match. Even her close family member confided to me that he didn't want to be around Teivel.

This same family member also told me Teivel had been a hypochondriac all of her life. He confided to me that Teivel had asked to live with him and his wife, but he could not allow her to live with them because she would never mind her own business.

So that was a revelation. My poor father had spent all of his time and energy running around trying to please this woman, and all she wanted was to leave him and live with her family member. In the end, she did not get her wish. She continually treated Dad like dirt, yelling at him constantly, according to the neighbours who hear everything, and clamming up only when visitors arrived.

Neighbours complained constantly about the yelling and screaming. That's why, finally, the family had to put Teivel into a nursing home. After she left the neighbours constantly asked me why Dad hadn't left her. They knew, when others didn't, about the terrible treatment he had suffered.

I had no answer for them. In the end, thank God, the decision was made for him, when her family moved her into the nursing home. In my opinion, it was the best thing to happen to our family in 37 years.

Teivel finally died on June 22, 2012. Needless to say, I did not shed any tears. Her family hushed up her passing. They were very secretive people, especially Teivel.

I was unable to get a full accounting of Teivel and Jack's joint accounts. The bank said that Teivel had probably opened and closed accounts over the years, and it would be almost impossible to trace.

I wondered where the money all went, all the money Dad had paid for each house. Teivel made no payments, but there was a house in her name. When they married, Dad also had a house of his own. My father also had a cottage, until he sold it.

In my opinion, she ferreted his money away and siphoned it off to her own family. Because of the matrimonial laws in Canada, I have no way to get the answers I want, but I'm sure the truth will come out sometime.

Meanwhile, based on the research I did while caring for my father's finances, I have very little doubt that is exactly what happened.

My father had been abused for so many years that he simply did whatever she demanded without question. In later years, she had rheumatoid arthritis and would not get out of bed. Due to a combination of my father's dementia, his poor upbringing which left his very child-like and these years of control and abuse, he could not defend himself against her. Even from her bed, she continued to yell at him and make demands.

In my opinion, she was evil, money hungry and unapproachable, calculating in every sense of the word. Just plain mean and selfish. In short, not much of a Christian.

Even after all of that, she still wanted more! She yelled and screamed, wanting more of my Great Aunt Margaret's inheritance. But Aunt Margaret was way too smart for her. Thank God for that!

~Chapter Seventeen~

'Through the years, I've read a number of self-help books, which I find enlightening about life in general. I've also read books about life-after-death, and several biographies.

Thanks to this reading, I've learned that it's okay to express yourself in the way that is right for you.

I read Barack Obama's biography, *Dreams from my Father, a Story of Race and Inheritance.* I liked the way he described places and people. It puts you right into the scene, you can see it in your mind's eye. Most of the famous people I've read about either are great writers, or they have great writers helping them with their work.

I find their stories so interesting, especially when they have risen from hardships, have been poor, or have suffered abuse or low self-esteem. It teaches me that we can do anything if we put our mind into to, especially if we accept there is a Higher Power.

I am grateful for the books I've read, and for the Higher Power that has guided me to read them. I'm grateful for the serenity I've found through my association with Al-Anon. Without it, I would have been lost.

I've been off anti-depressants since April 27, 2013, and I feel fine. After the exhaustion of caring for my father, I'd had to go on the medication. It was just too much for me.

Now, I have no anxiety at all, and I am sleeping well.

I was seeing a counsellor and she was great. Last time I saw her, she pointed out I'd been visiting her for a year.

I couldn't believe it. To me, it sure didn't seem that long. Could it be I still have a lot to talk to her about?

When my counsellor confided to me that her husband had been brought up JW, I was shocked, both that he'd been brought up in the cult, and that she'd told me about it. Apparently, he had also been deeply affected by growing up that way.

The first thing I thought was that I'm not alone!

For some reason, we always assume we are the only ones who suffer in our particular way. Of course, this is far from true. But the isolationist way we are raised in the JW adds to that feeling of being the only one.

When I moved, I had to stop seeing that counsellor. I'm looking for someone closer to where I live.

There have been a lot of changes in my life recently, many of them good. On May 31, 2013 I moved into a family member's house. This was a huge change, and I lived there for about a year.

Recently, I've been reading *Codependent No More: How to Stop Controlling Others and Start Caring for Yourself*, by Melody Beattie. I'm fascinated by her perspective, and thinking a lot about her advice. She gives very detailed insight on the problem and how to change it. For starters, as with anything, you have to first realize it is a problem. That's a big first step. If you can't see what you're doing, you can't change it.

It took me a long time to see what I was doing wrong. This book shows me how to change the actions, and how the change will benefit both me and the codependent.

I believe I learned the codependent behaviour from my mother without ever knowing it. There is care, and there is codependency, and they are not the same. They will never mix.

When I finish the book, I'll know much more about myself and how to care for myself in a much better way.

It was on the advice of my counsellor that I started reading this book. She was sure right, it's educational and easy to understand.

I wonder what else will occur to me as I continue reading this book.

A friend of mine once told me that reading non-fiction is a type of therapy. So in a way I'm taking care of myself even as I read.

There are many people who believe that, after a certain age, we should not bother trying to learn and grow.

I once had to take an interview with a teacher for a Personal Support Worker Certificate course. The teacher asked me if I didn't think maybe I was a little too old to take the course. She told me the course was intense, and might be too much for me.

I hardly blinked an eye. I told her I was strong, had basically nothing wrong with me physically, and that the employment office had suggested that I take this course.

I'd already passed the pre-requisite test on July 4.

The teacher reminded me that if I was absent for 3 days, I'd be removed from the course. She asked me if I had back problems. I didn't. The gist of her tone and words was that I should not try.

I knew I could do it, so long as I got funding and an okay from my doctor, plus all the immunizations needed.

"One day at a time!" I told myself.

The teacher was trying to convince me I'd have a hard time getting work in the P.S.W. program at my age. I told her I didn't believe that was true, as I'd already worked for two companies that could have hired me, if I'd had the training.

Ultimately, the teacher approved me for the course.

I met with my doctor on July 8, and later that day discussed the course with my counsellor.

I also needed approval for funding from the employment company who had referred me.

There turned out to be a problem regarding the funding, and because I live in Pickering, I would only qualify for half of the funding we'd discussed.

After reading *Codependent No More*, I have a number of questions I'd like to ask my counsellor. In the book, it says don't do anything you don't want to do. It's like my yin and yang are fighting against each other. Part of me wants to do the course, because it came to me out of the blue. I've passed the test and the interview. Also, when I take this course I'll be able to obtain my grade 12 equivalency, which will be a bonus. The course is only for five months, and after that I can choose where I want to work, and it will increase my earning ability. I really do need the additional money.

Also, anything you do or learn in this life is never wasted, according to the book I'm reading. Of course, I already knew that, but I'm not sure I ever really believed it.

I'd forgotten how good it is to have a goal. I'd put my own goals on the back burner for a long time. As I write this page, I still don't know whether I'll take this course. A lot will depend on things I can't control, like what will happen tomorrow, what the course times will be. Sometimes all we can do is wait and see. I now understand that, whatever decision I make, it will be for my Highest and Best Good, and will be what is meant to be.

I cannot control these things. In this life, I am only a messenger.

I have given up my power to the God of my understanding. He alone controls everything. I've had to "Let Go and Let God" in every part of my life. I've realized that I am not able to control things, and I thank God for that, because my life before this realization was unmanageable.

I had to take my focus off the alcoholic in my life and put it back onto me. Look where I am now thanks to this simple action!

I'm now serene, I have a sense of serenity and am in a much better place than I could ever have dreamed, all because I "Let Go and Let God" take control of my life, both spiritually and mentally. Next, I have to work on the physical, and with God's help I'll be able to improve that as well!

I believe it's important to keep a balance in life.

Well, now for the update that was promised. I passed the test and the interview, and am now enrolled in the Personal Support Worker Course to earn my certificate. I've also completed my grade 12 English course and exam, and my grade 12 math and exam. I did well in English. I completed these courses in the summer before beginning the PSW course in the fall.

Yesterday, I was at a small café in Ajax, where I saw a sign advertising a 20 minute psychic reading for $20.00. I was hooked and decided to get a reading.

The lady told me I'll do well in the course, but I won't get a job in this field. Instead I'll use the knowledge to help people I know, family members and situations that might arise.

The lady also predicted that I would write, and that the only things stopping me were procrastination and a title for my book. She advised me to ask my Spirit Guides and Higher Power for help.

The psychic also advised me to write lists of what I hope to accomplish with my book. She said I could do anything I wanted, and that I'm very intuitive.

She reminded me to let go of my fear, and my need for control. To just sit down and let the pen do the writing, so that is what I'm doing.

This book is about my life. How I got here, the journey, the lessons, the hardships, and how I came out on top by following a Power greater than myself.

The psychic predicted all of this before I started my course. I had started writing this book in January of 2013, but had not mentioned a word about the book to the psychic.

She also said I'd reached a point where it was important to enjoy my life. She said I should not take on new tasks of caring for others, that I have too much to complete for myself, and I'm to look after that.

I am likely going to buy a condo or rent an apartment in this area in two years.

She also predicted that I'd take a trip in the spring!

It will be interesting to see if what she predicted comes true!

It's now September 3, 2013, the day I start my PSW Course. It's also my Great-Aunt Margaret's birthday. I'm up early, probably due to nervous energy and anticipation of the day ahead.

I'm concerned about where we're going to have lunch today, whether I should pack lunch or go out. There's not much writing time this morning, so I'll have to write later!

As it turned out, the course and exams placement kept me so busy there was no time at all to devote to writing.

On Sept. 7, 2013, we are planning a surprise birthday party for my brother's 60th birthday. It will be on the Empress Boat in Toronto Harbour. A dinner cruise. I think it will be so much fun, and I'd like to do it again on my 65th!

I resume my writing on Saturday, March 8, 2014. I've now completed the PSW Course. I also completed my grade 12 diploma. All I needed was the English and Math to earn my diploma. You have no idea how much satisfaction this simple thing has given me!

It was an intense course and I worked very hard. After completing I worked at two placements, one in a nursing home and the other in a group home. Pretty good for a 63 year-old lady, eh?

My brother had rented a double trailer home in Florida in a gated community and invited me to join him for two weeks. It was a chance to spend time with him and to do a few things together, as well as to escape the extremely cold winter we were having.

It was the worst winter I could remember, and the most snow. It was really hard to return home from Florida. A few days after I got home, my Aunt Helen died, on February 21, 2014. She was my mother's eldest sister, 95 years old and a lovely lady. I'll miss her a great deal. Her passing left a real void in my life. I'm grateful for the time we had together and hope to see her again if there is an afterlife.

The funeral was on March 6. Her daughter Marilyn wrote a beautiful eulogy, describing her mother's life. I hope to get a copy of it. It honoured her mother in a way most mothers would want, including myself.

My childhood memories involve a lot of isolation, growing up in the JW society. It revolved around meetings, Bible Studies, conventions, preaching the Good News door-to-door. My parents didn't know any other way to raise me and they thought they were doing the right thing.

In my opinion, there are a lot of better ways to raise children, ways that do not isolate them and their families. No one religion or cult has the right to dictate to people how to thing, act, or how to live. I believe these cults brainwash people by making them listen to the same messages over and over again, and by isolating them from everyone else in the larger community.

I do not believe there is any one right religion. I believe God is there for you wherever you are. You do not have to attend church to get that help. No one really knows what happens when we die. We all hope our spirit goes on forever, but there's no way, while alive, to know for sure.

Since no one has returned from the dead to tell us, it's all up in the air. What will be, will be. It's in God's hands and He or She is the only Being we have to answer to.

I do believe in a Higher Power, but I do not believe you have to go to a church or a Kingdom Hall in order to talk to God. All you have to do is to ask for help, to speak openly to God when you need help, and when you are ready to receive it.

I am a witness to this belief. It has happened to me. I've received help when I most needed it. I've learned that sometimes it's best to do nothing, to take no action. Wait, listen, and the answer will come to you. Sometimes it's better to wait than to rush into a decision without really thinking. Often you will regret the hastily made decision.

Many of the self-help books and biographies I've read have also enlightened me with this same message. Many have theories about the after-life. I've discovered both good and bad in many different religions. None are perfect, and none know everything.

Let's face it, we all have only one Judge. We are not meant to judge our fellow-men. When at last we are six feet under, we will discover the truth about whether there is an after-life, a judgement day.

Our only mission is this: to do our best to be a good person and to follow the golden rule. There isn't much more to it than that.

Life would not be such an exciting journey if we all knew everything. I remind myself of this constantly. No one knows everything, and no one is perfect. But the Jehovah's Witnesses seem to imply that they *do* know everything, and they are close to perfection as well, and that they have the Only True Religion.

I say poppycock, bologna! This is just not true.

I must add that, since writing these pages, I've found the greatest sense of contentment as well as a lot of fulfillment.

Writing has also helped me to realize something else: the nature of my upbringing may be the reason I feel most comfortable alone. Because I was raised that way, isolated. I do enjoy other people's company. However, I believe I use self-isolation as a means of protection, and I only realized this today.

I used to work so hard at protecting myself from hurt, injury, from other people. However, what I didn't see when I was younger is that if you work so hard to protect yourself, you are not really living your life.

I definitely want to begin living my life without isolation.

Everyone needs quiet times now and again. But far greater than that is our need for people, places and things. You can't control others, and you don't need to control them. Just enjoy them.

This is the essence of Al-Anon in a nutshell. You must be open to that. Once you are open to it, the world is your oyster. You don't need religious doctrines, just a sense of self and an openness to a Higher Power greater than yourself, that you can lean on at all times, and where you can turn for guidance in your daily life.

A Power you can rely on not just in times of trouble, but every single day. One day at a time.

This is what I've come to believe. I follow the twelve-step program and the twelve traditions and the golden rule. The golden rule is "Do unto others as you would have them do unto you." These principles have given me a sense of peace and forgiveness to my fellow-men, something I didn't have or understand before I found Al-Anon and the AA meetings.

It takes working the steps, attending meetings, service work and spending spiritual time with my Higher Power, something I never took the time for in my old life.

I did believe in God, but I never allowed myself to rely on His or Her Higher Power. When I did pray, it was because someone told me to. I thought you were supposed to pray when you wanted something, and not on a regular basis. When I used to pray, I really did not think God could help me.

Now, everything is different. When I pray, I ask my Higher Power to show me what he would like me to do, and I seek guidance in different ways. If no answer comes to me then I do nothing. In other words, I ask my

Higher Power what I should do, and what is in my best interest to do.

I now enjoy a relationship with my Higher Power or God every day. I guess you could say I had a spiritual awakening in the fact I now rely on God, how He directs me, which I never had in the days before Al-Anon. I've let go of my anxiety. I used to be aware of it in my chest constantly. I have greater confidence in myself. I've grown to love God in a way I never knew I could.

It is a constant, abiding love that stems from meditating, reading and following a day-to-day course to keep me in tune with this.

Like anything else, if you don't keep doing these things, you will lose them. That's why I kept returning to Al-Anon. I try to keep my life simple and live each day one day at a time.

On March 25, 2014 I told my financial advisor I was going to retire, based on what he told me. I also decided to keep driving my car, and not to exchange it for a new one.

I made these decisions, major life changing decisions, for myself. I feel it's best for me right now. God willing, they will prove to be good decisions, but there is no way of knowing.

One day at a time.

At least retirement will give me more time to write, to travel, to look after myself and stay happy, healthy, and maybe even wealthy in the long run. Only time will tell!

The psychic I consulted told me not to be afraid, to make my own decisions. That roadblocks were holding me back, and that I was better off making my own decisions and to write about my journey, my decisions and the outcomes. Part of taking that journey is being able to handle any mistakes I might make along the way.

I think this is what she was trying to say to me, and so this is what I'm doing.

She seemed to me to be an honest psychic. I appreciated her honesty with me.

It's another cold winter day. I'll be attending an Al-Anon meeting tonight. Another group will be chairing the meeting so it will be interesting.

Just before I began my five-month Personal Support Worker course, I stopped attending my Al-Anon meetings. The course was just too intense and there was no time or energy for anything else.

It seems we need different things at different times in our lives. I found myself drifting from the Al-Anon meetings. They were not giving me the same as they had before. Although I may not attend, I can still pray for guidance, and keep the focus on myself, which I am doing.

I only know I'm trying to follow my instincts and see where they lead. I know the program works if you work it. I have a new understanding of addictions and the people who suffer from addiction. I better understand the dynamics between addicts and their families.

Religion is an addiction. That's something I learned on my journey. No one is perfect, and it never hurts to ask for help along the way. I've learned a lot, and still have a lot to learn. That's the way life is.

I hope you can appreciate my journey for what it is, and what it has been, and I hope you've learned something, too.

~Chapter Eighteen~

I believe it was the spring of 2014 when I began looking for a new place to live. I'd finished my course, but had not yet gone to Florida to visit my brother.

I'd put an offer on a house in Port Perry. But the home inspection revealed the house was a money pit and not worth purchasing. This was just one of many things that had not worked out, including another place in Port Perry and a few in Lindsay.

I just could not seem to find a place that was affordable and right for me.

A friend of mine had even been looking and had found a couple of places in Lagoon City, but nothing was right. I was becoming really discouraged and so was my whole family. They were giving me their two cents, which was not helping.

I finally found a cute two-bedroom two-bathroom house in the small town of Lindsay and had put in an offer. But I realized when it came down to the wire, no matter what I might do with this place or how perfect it was, I didn't want to live somewhere where the only person I knew was the realtor.

So my friend Dianne and I went to a Tim Horton's where I broke down and said I couldn't go through with the purchase. I just didn't feel comfortable buying that place, or any place so far away.

I wanted a place in Scarborough, and might be able to afford it, but it would have to be a condo, not a house, because as a suburb of Toronto, Scarborough prices were going up all the time.

I told my realtor I wanted to change to someone who specialized in condos, who would have a good knowledge of what was available, which she didn't have. I wanted a condo in a good area, one that would hold its value. She put me in touch with another realtor that worked for her same company, this way my first realtor would still earn a percentage of the purchase, since she'd been working with me a long time.

I was so frustrated and discouraged and thought I would never find a place. I had put in two more offers that didn't work out. So, on June 20, I told my realtor that if the condo search did not work out, I was going to stop searching until the fall. The realtor agreed, but she said she really thought the latest condo she suggested was going to be "the one", so we set out to go look at it.

I remember the realtor driving us up to the entrance, and I was thinking how beautiful all the flowers were in the gardens. I reminded myself not to get ahead of myself, to wait and see what the inside of the condo looked like before getting excited.

So we entered the condo.

It was beautifully decorated, so clean and bright. The halls were well lit and clean. Again I thought this was a welcome change, but don't get too excited. Wait to see what the actual condo looks like!

Well, we entered and I got a pleasant surprise! It was bright and clean inside and had a huge patio. Everything was neutral. The kitchen was updated, and even though it was a one-bedroom, the bedroom was huge and apparently the building had guest suites if you had company staying over, with separate facilities and gas heat.

Gas heat was proving very difficult to find. Everywhere I went, all I found was places with electric heat, which is very expensive. This condo had been a seniors' condo since 2001 and you did not have to pay the GST until you sold the unit.

Everyone seemed very friendly. The grounds were beautiful and you felt like you were in the country, because the place was hidden near a golf course. It overlooked the golf course, so there would be no additional building taking place. Also, the building was only six floors high, not a high rise, and it was not far from any of my family members.

Best of all, the place had come down in price, as the owners were anxious to get a cash deal. It was within my price range and seemed to have everything I wanted. Of course, I thought it might be too good to be true. The realtor suggested I should put in an offer right away if I wanted the place.

So I did and they accepted it!

They also wanted a short closing date, which I was able to offer them.

I moved into my new place on July 7, 2014. Everything worked out, like it was meant to be!

One interesting aspect was that I had come full circle, in a way. My new place was very near to the home where I had been raised as a child and teenager. So, after all the moves I'd made in my life, I was right back where I'd started. Somewhere I never thought I would find myself again!

It struck me as unusual: I'd been sort of running away from my past all of my adult life, and now I ended up confronting it, without realizing it, and in more ways than one.

My grandson offered to help me with the move, even though I'd hired movers. I was grateful for the support and we went out to lunch afterward. He is a very considerate and caring young man.

I'd taken several loads to the new place in my car before the official date. Because the new place was on ground level, it made the whole job much easier.

On one trip, a lady greeted me with a small banana bread she had baked as a welcoming gift. She thought I would be hungry with all the work I was doing. I thought that was awfully nice of her. I soon learned she was a busy bee in the condo, between looking after the annual garage sale and hosting coffee hours and helping with regular pot luck dinners.

There was also a greeter in the building, who told you about the hall monitors who had been assigned in case of fire, and who the monitor was for my floor. Two ladies brought me a plant and welcomed me to the building. I found it to be very nice and personable.

Devi was the first person I spoke to when I arrived at the building. She was working in the garden, and we instantly became friends. I felt like I'd known her for years!

It was going to be great finally moving into my own place, after sharing a space with my family members in their house for a year. It was time to move. I was ready, and so were they.

On July 7, 2014, it finally happened!

In the beginning of June 2015, a friend was having a hard time with her mother. The mom was in a nursing home, and was dying. My friend's sister-in-law, whom I'd met on a couple of occasions, was in bad shape. She had cancer and my friend could not leave her mother to travel to Florida to help her sister-in-law.

My friend told me that looking after her sister-in-law should be easy and her place was spotless. Her sister-in-law, she assured me, could wash herself, feed herself, and my friend said I was the only one she could trust to do a good job. She couldn't tell me how long I would be needed in Florida, but it was just to be until her mother passed away.

My friend told me my flights would be paid for, and I would receive between $800 and $1000 per week. However, she could not say for how long.

Also, I knew that as a caregiver, you need to have someone else relieve you no matter how easy the position is. After no more than three days, you need to have someone take over for you.

However, there was not going to be any relief for me, I alone would be looking after the person. To help my friend, I agreed to do it.

My family advised against it, saying it was too much work, but I didn't listen. I was feeling good, and wasn't thinking clearly and wanted to help Dianne, who is a good person and a good friend.

I talked myself into doing it, since Dianne did not expect her mother to last very long, and I had the impression Dianne would be taking over from me very shortly.

When I arrived, it was late at night. I hadn't eaten for quite a while. The lady I was to be helping picked me up in her neighbour's car and drove us to her home.

There was nothing to eat in the house. The lady informed me her friend would be picking us up early the next day to take us to her first treatment, an experimental treatment. This was why she needed my help; her doctor would not implement the new treatment unless she could guarantee someone would stay with her. She had exhausted every other form of treatment, and this was her last option.

Either she could not find good help in Florida, or she didn't want to pay, or she couldn't afford to pay. I suspect she couldn't afford to pay, since it was my friend who was paying me. I had found that to be kind of odd.

Although I was exhausted, I tried to stay awake and keep an eye on the lady, since she was using oxygen. It was lucky I'd kept an eye on her, as the tube fell out of her nose. I rushed to replace it.

Morning came much too soon, and with very little sleep and very little to eat, our ride arrived on time to take us to the center for treatment. She had to take the treatment for five straight days, then off for one or two days. This was the process.

Unfortunately, she turned out to be the patient from hell. She was used to doing everything for herself and doing everything her way. She had been in control her whole life, and didn't want to give up any control.

Even though she was very sick, weighing only 91 lbs, and standing five-feet-ten-inches. She looked terrible, all skin and bones and very weak.

In short, no matter how diplomatic I tried to be, she didn't want to be told what to do. It was meant for her own good, but she didn't see it that way. For example, she insisted on smoking in the bathroom with her oxygen tank on.

I couldn't make her happy, no matter how I tried. Nothing I cooked was good enough.

After only two weeks, I knew it was too much. I had to get out of there or go completely crazy.

To make things worse, Dianne's mother had passed away. Before she died, my friend had planned a small memorial, no big deal. But suddenly, after she died, my friend's aunt (her mother's sister) wanted to come to the memorial. Because she was so old and had a bad heart, she had to get the okay from her family doctor before she could book a flight.

I understood, but as I had already told Dianne, things were not going well in Florida and I needed to return home.

I'd tried to be patient, saying nothing until her mother died and trying to hold on. However, I could not handle the situation much longer.

Dianne promised to book me a flight home, but didn't follow through. So I knew I would have to take the bull by the horns. I booked my own flight out of there. I told my friend she could reimburse me later, but I couldn't wait any longer.

Dianne suggested someone I could call to maybe get a better deal on the flight, but that didn't work out. So in the end, I decided to call the number on my original ticket, and I was able to book the return flight through them. I was given the last seat on a flight leaving Florida the following evening.

I forgot to mention that the flights were only once each week, so if I hadn't booked immediately, I would have been stuck another week.

I'm not joking or exaggerating when I say that, if I'd been held captive there another week, I would have ended up in a psychiatric hospital for sure. I could feel a mental breakdown coming on, and I had to take care of myself right away.

I returned home physically and emotionally exhausted. My friend Dianne insisted on picking me up at Toronto International Airport. I could hardly speak to her on the drive home, I felt so bad.

Dianne also felt bad, that I'd been so mistreated by her relative.

I told her we'd both made a mistake. I should have known better, and should not have accepted the position. She said she should not have asked me.

I reassured her it would not affect our friendship, and I'm pleased to say that it hasn't.

That night I went to bed exhausted. I'd called my naturopath, who had advised me of a product I could buy in Florida to relax me, but she had also told me the best remedy was to get out of the situation. My brother Ken and another good friend, Devi, had also encouraged me to return home.

As soon as I got home, I tried to get an appointment with my naturopath, but she didn't have an opening for two weeks, so I went to sleep as best I could.

The next morning I woke to the sound of my phone ringing. It was my friend, Devi. She asked me if I was all right. I said I was not too good, and I started to cry.

Devi asked if I'd called our naturopath. I told her about the two week wait for an appointment.

She said to leave it with her. She would call the naturopath and tell her I could not wait two weeks – that would be too late.

She also told me she'd had a bad dream about me, in which I had been crying. That's how she knew I was in trouble.

Needless to say, I was flabbergasted!

Devi called again to say she'd gotten me an emergency appointment. She said to get showered and ready, and she would take me that morning to the naturopath.

The naturopath sold me a lot of products to get my health back. She insisted I needed a full month's rest, and to take everything she had suggested. She said if I followed her instructions, I'd be okay in a month's time.

I did, and in a month I was on my feet again, in good shape.

If it hadn't been for Devi's quick action, I could well have fallen very ill, and maybe even been in much worse shape for much longer than I was. With her keen knowledge, intuition and response to the situation, I got better quickly.

Devi is a very trusted, selfless good friend. One in a million!

I made up my mind never to try to look after anyone in those circumstances again.

I'd like to add an observation here. Even though I did very well in the Personal Support Worker course, and had a real aptitude for getting along with the elderly, and even though I did very well in my placements, I found that looking after the elderly in the nursing home was depressing. I didn't seem to be able to leave my work at work. I found it draining, and brought my worries for my patients home with me.

It's a necessary skill in life, to be able to survive. It's really important not to take your work home with you.

In early May, 2016, I went on a trip to Glasgow, Scotland. I went on a partial private tour to Edinburgh Castle, Dumfries, Dumfriesshire and Canonbie, where my Great Aunt Margaret and I had traced our roots. I met with a couple that had bought the Barclay Castle (Towie Barclay Castle) in the early '70s. They had restored the castle, and they live in it to this day. The castle is located where my paternal grandmother's family originated. Their name was spelled Barclaigh, Berkeley and many other variations through the centuries. We were able to trace them back to 1153 in Turniff, Aberdeenshire, Scotland, a place I never thought I would see, as it is a private home.

But luck was on my side. By Googling private tours in Scotland, I ended up having a life-changing experience. This lovely couple gave me their Barclay Family Tree, dating back to the original Barclays who had actually built and lived in the castle.

Now, my challenge will be to try to connect the information Aunt Margaret and I already had with the information these kind people shared with me.

Their only request was that I not use any of their photos from the Internet, and I said I would not.

For me, this was an unbelievable experience, one I never imagined.

It reminded me of the movie *A Field of Dreams*. Kevin Costner says "If I build it, they will come." This is what happened, these people restored the castle, and now many descendants of the Barclay Clan come to visit and to see their roots.

Before I went to Scotland, there were a lot of little signs pointing me in that direction. For example, two cheques arrived in the mail that were totally unexpected. Also, I got a large income tax refund. These occurrences convinced me I was meant to go, as I could do so without taking any money out of my investments, which were dwindling.

I know it sounds weird, but I believe the universe was telling me that traveling to Scotland was the right thing to do.

I believe the universe guides us at times. For example, I had lunch a while ago with a friend I hadn't seen for years. She told me about her sister, who was running an Indie publishing company and might be able to help publish my book. I felt it was a clear sign that I should continue and complete my writing. I felt it was both a sign and a gift I could not ignore.

I could add, "God works in mysterious ways."

I'd like to end this book with a few words about my current self. I'm a strong, independent woman. I live alone, and do not feel lonely.

For the most part, I enjoy peace and harmony in my life. I am fortunate to have a grandson, a very special person. He is an old soul, very responsible and mature for his age. I feel extremely gifted to have him in my life.

My message to readers is simple. Never forget that life is about learning. Be open to learning new things and to exploring new possibilities in your life!

I'd like to send a special dedication to anyone who has been abused in their life, whether the abuse was emotional, physical, sexual or financial. Also, to anyone with addictions, whether to substances or to emotional drains such as religion. And finally to anyone suffering from depression or dyslexia, because you are a fighter. You are forced to work harder than most, just to maintain an equilibrium or balance in your everyday life.

Never forget: You are not alone. If you need help, it is out there waiting for you. You need only go and look for it. Remain open to the possibility of a Higher Power, and to any avenue of help you may encounter. You don't need to attend a church to find peace and contentment.

Slogans I live by, learned at Al-Anon:

> *Seek, and you will find.*
> *If there's a will, there is a way.*
> *One day at a time.*
> *Keep it simple*

Sincerely,
Gail Louise (Sharpe) Kelly
A Survivor

About the Author

Gail Kelly was born in 1950 and raised in Toronto, Canada. After many moves she has returned to her hometown. She has come full circle both by her physical move and more generally in her life. She is a mother of two grown sons and a grandmother of one grown grandson. She is also a sister and an aunt.

She enjoys traveling and is planning to travel somewhere different in the next few years.

Gail returned to school at the age of 63 to complete her Grade 12, earning her diploma, and completed a five month Advanced Course to become a Personal Support Worker. She was the eldest in the class in 2013, the youngest student being 21. Gail has received a diploma for attending Centennial College, in the 2 year course in Home Furnishings and Fashion Merchandising at Centennial College, as well as a one year Certificate course at Sheridan College to become a florist. Gail designed and hand painted ceramics as a ceramic artist and sold her art for 25 years, since 1979.

Gail has worn many hats during her life time, from florist assistant to model home decorator at Eaton's.

She has been a volunteer for Centennial Hospital, Scouts and Girl Guides.

Gail worked cleaning for the elderly for sixteen years and also worked as a Companion for the elderly.

This is her first book, one she felt she had to write to show how this Jehovah's Witness religious cult had affected her and her family's life. In spite of it all, she has overcome such devastation and tragedy.